Osmo Vänskä

Orchestra Builder

Osmo Vänskä

Orchestra Builder

Text by Michael Anthony

Photography by Greg Helgeson and Ann Marsden

Leonard Flachman, Editor

Kirk House Publishers

Minneapolis, Minnesota

Osmo Vänskä
Orchestra Builder

Leonard Flachman, Editor
Text by Michael Anthony
Photography: Greg Helgeson, Ann Marsden, and others (see page 127)
Cover Photo: Ann Marsden
Editing and Design: Karen Walhof

Library of Congress Cataloging-in-Publication Data
  Osmo Vänskä : orchestra builder / Leonard Flachman, editor ; text by Michael Anthony.
    p. cm.
    ISBN-13: 978-1-933794-20-4 (hardbound)
    ISBN-10: 1-933794-20-8 (hardbound)
    1. Vänskä, Osmo, 1953- 2. Conductors (Music)—Biography. 3. Minnesota Orchestra. I. Anthony, Michael, 1942- II. Flachman, Leonard.
    ML422.V36O86 2009
    784.2092~dc22
    [B]
            2009016890

Kirk House Publishers, PO Box 390759, Minneapolis, MN 55439 (www.kirkhouse.com)
Manufactured by Regal Printing in Hong Kong

Table of Contents

Foreword

Osmo Vänskä's arrival at the Minnesota Orchestra came at a time when the orchestra was searching for its real identity. Could the new music director bring out the orchestra's excellent qualities, some of which resided just below the surface? Could he entice the musicians to work willingly at the push and pull involved in reaching a new, high level of playing, so consistently superb that it would solidify the Minnesota Orchestra's position on the top rung of American orchestras—even elevate it to the rank of famed international ensembles? Would he draw the attention of major critics to focus on this orchestra in the heartland? In each case, the elements of success appeared to be at hand.

Osmo faced tall tasks on the local front as well. If he led the orchestra to new heights of performance excellence and into the national and international spotlight, would attendance skyrocket at home? The community here has experienced years of cutbacks in school music education—unlike Osmo's native Finland, where music is key to each child's education, and classical music is an integral part of culture. Given this educational gap, would he be able to attract younger audiences to concerts? If so, would they return as readily as mature audiences? How could—and would—Osmo become a part of the fabric of the community on this side of the ocean?

Osmo and his wife Pirkko bought a condo on the Mississippi River in downtown Minneapolis and firmly established residency. Osmo made it clear from the beginning that this was home, even if their adult children and a beloved "granddog" were staying in Finland. Neighbors became accustomed to seeing him jogging around the neighborhood, buying groceries at Lunds, attending plays at the Guthrie and in summer merging into traffic on his motorcycle.

Osmo has approached his personal and musical life with a measured style, revealing facets of himself that would have been hard to anticipate. He took up the clarinet again, first playing at a Symphony Ball, then at Sommerfest and with various Twin Cities ensembles, at the Mostly Mozart Festival in New York City, and in Napa Valley venues. He turned up at the Dakota, a famed local jazz club, to jam with local artists as well as Minnesota Orchestra musicians after concerts. Not to be outdazzled by Doc Severinsen, the Minnesota Orchestra's pops conductor laureate, Osmo appeared at sold-out concerts conducting the music of ABBA in an elaborately styled outfit that left no doubt about his sense of humor or his readiness to go the extra mile when the music invited it.

He didn't shy away from attending and supporting other arts events and organizations across the Twin Cities. When MacPhail Center for Music, a venerable music education institution, launched a capital campaign, he stepped forward with a contribution; a clarinet studio now bears his name. On touring the completed MacPhail facility, so impressed was he with the acoustics in its performance space that he chose it as the venue for a Minnesota Orchestra chamber music series.

Many artists, whether they're painters, sculptors, writers, or musicians, find in their lives a closeness to nature and to the divine. Osmo experiences this connection as well as inspiration and peace on his long motorcycle rides across the Finnish countryside and along the byways of rural Minnesota. The instrument for his latest forays into composing may be a pen, but his revelations come at least partially from the energy and sense of freedom he derives from these excursions.

In conversation, Osmo is intense and committed. He wants music to be available to everyone. He has said he'll play any music so long as it is good music. He has also said it would take time for him to establish trust with audiences. That trust now being in place, he has tested us at times with difficult repertoire. His wry sense of humor, often evident in rehearsals, was directed at me one evening when I boldly proclaimed that "Kalevi Aho's Symphony No. 10 was an assault on one's ears." He responded with a twinkle in his eye, "But it is good music."

Osmo has continued to reveal himself. But even for those of us who think we know him quite well, he remains intriguing, challenging our minds and stimulating our senses—all the while demanding the best of himself and his musicians.

It has been a terrific ride with rave reviews—from Minneapolis to London, from New York to Vienna and many points between. For his tremendous accomplishments, in 2004 Osmo was recognized by Musical America as Conductor of the Year. In 2008, closer to home, the University of Minnesota conferred on him an honorary doctorate of humane letters. The accompanying citation spoke volumes about Osmo's role here. It referenced his dedication to young composers, with whom he works closely as they learn about the business of composing at the orchestra's Composer Institute. It also recognized his substantial personal commitment to the Minnesota Orchestra's multifaceted collaboration with the University of Minnesota School of Music. David Myers, director of the University's School of Music, called the honorary degree "a fitting tribute to Maestro Vänskä, who has dedicated his life to music education and has infused his singular spirit into the cultural life of Minnesota." Kathy Romey, an associate professor who is also director of the University's choral activities, was equally laudatory, describing Osmo as "a person who continues to serve society through his art with commitment, passion, humility, and integrity."

Six seasons into his Minnesota tenure, it is clear that while Osmo Vänskä has indeed led the Minnesota Orchestra into a new golden era artistically, he also has fully embraced his new American community in the Midwest. His community returns that embrace: Osmo *is* the conductor and music director for whom we had hoped.

Nicky B. Carpenter, Board of Directors, Life Director
Minnesota Orchestral Association

Preface

The project of writing at length about a living person has difficulties with which the biographer of a long-dead figure need not contend. The life story, first of all, is unfinished. The most telling event or project, the one that will alter forever the world's view of the subject might be just around the corner, announced just a day or two after the book is published. (In fact, just before this manuscript was completed, Osmo and his wife Pirkko announced that they were divorcing after thirty-five years.) The advantage of writing about a living person is access to the subject, not just letters and e-mails but actual face-to-face conversation. At the very least, the writer gets the subject's view of events, and that is surely part of the story.

The interviews with Osmo Vänskä for this book took place between July 2008 and February 2009 at his office in Orchestra Hall in Minneapolis. Osmo doesn't mind talking about himself, about his past, his experiences at the podium, and especially his ideas about music.

At each of the eleven hour-long interviews, Osmo thought hard about every question he was asked. Richard D. Lewis, author of *Finland, Cultural Lone Wolf*, says that's a Finnish trait. Finns don't speak and think at the same time. If they're asked a question, they will think a while first, then answer.

Others, of course, contributed to this Vänskä story: dozens of people in Finland—musicians, family members, journalists, colleagues, friends; a few more in England; and staff, musicians, and board members of the Minnesota Orchestra. All were forthcoming. The book is largely a positive portrait of a positive individual. To be sure, there have been dark moments in Osmo's life—a few—and he speaks about those. At one point, for instance, his career seemed to be moving at the pace of an elderly snail going uphill, and he became discouraged, even though he likes to think of himself as an optimist. But he persevered, either because that's his nature or because, being a Finn, he has what his countrymen call *sisu*, which means gumption or stamina or fortitude, and eventually his career began to take off, first in Europe and then in the United States.

At the time of this writing, Osmo was in his mid-50s—young for a conductor. Many conductors do their best work after the age of sixty. Given Osmo's vigorous good health, it's likely he will be waving his arms in front of orchestras for decades to come.

Michael Anthony

Introduction

Osmo Vänskä is one of the most compelling and admired conductors of our time. Born in Finland in 1953, he spent a number of years as a professional clarinetist and embodies the values of modesty, team-work, persistent effort, and strong religious faith. He claims that he never expected a huge international career but simply wanted, from his earliest days, to conduct and do the best he could do. He brings a unique power and delicacy to the music he conducts. He cites his devotion to the composer, and he is fastidious, even obsessive, in his fidelity to the scores in front of him. The effect, at its best, on recordings and in concerts, is a re-invention of the music, the offering of a new and fresh experience of something we realize we didn't know as well as we thought. Vänskä's recordings of the music of Jean Sibelius with the Lahti (Finland) Symphony Orchestra for the Swedish BIS Records label are at times icy and bleak in their refusal to sentimentalize. His Beethoven, much applauded, is brisk, tight, fiery, and strongly accented. His Carl Nielsen symphonies have character and bite. And conspicuous in his vast repertoire is the work of contemporary Finnish composers—Kalevi Aho, Uuno Klami, Einojuhani Rautavaara, Jonas Kokkonen—none of whom would have reached their current renown without Vänskä's support.

Vänskä achieved his current stature slowly. As chief conductor of the Lahti Symphony Orchestra, he remained largely unknown outside Finland. It was the much-acclaimed Lahti recordings, starting in the early 1990s, that exposed the Vänskä name to a wider public. In 1996, while retaining his title in Lahti, he took over the BBC Scottish Symphony Orchestra as chief conductor and became a favorite of audiences and critics throughout Great Britain. Eventually expanding to America in 2002, he became the acclaimed music director of the Minnesota Orchestra.

Though Vänskä is in great demand as a guest conductor in both the United States and Europe, his career suggests that his strongest work comes through a lengthy and intense relationship with a single orchestra. There is a musical reason for this: Vänskä's formidable work ethic. ("Verk, verk, verk" has become a catch phrase among musicians at the Minnesota Orchestra.) He is a true orchestra builder, relentless in rehearsal. His ideas of sound and his demands for precision take time to develop—years, in fact. But there is a sociological reason, also: Vänskä's strong sense of community. For him,

Osmo is an orchestra builder, relentless in rehearsal.

music has a social function. It brings people together. It can bind a city, and it can bind a nation. An orchestra, in Vänskä's view, is a community, and the conductor is only first among equals. But Vänskä takes it further. He believes music can console, it can uplift, it can tell us the truth about our lives—dark truths as well as those that comfort. It can, as he has said, cleanse the soul, chiefly because—and here is the idea that sustains and energizes him—music is a gift from God.

Vänskä's music-making, with its focus on rhythmic precision, wide dynamic range, and fierce energy, is easier to characterize than the man himself. The contradictions loom large. For instance this is a man in a celebrity profession who claims to be embarrassed by the trappings of stardom, a sober Lutheran who drives a motorcycle, wears leather when he does so and is probably right when he proclaims, "I'm wilder than my image." He is a conductor of patently serious intent who once walked onstage at Orchestra Hall in Minneapolis wearing a 1970s outfit in the style of Sonny Bono to conduct an evening of songs by ABBA—and really enjoyed himself.

He usually speaks with certainty concerning musical issues, as if these are matters he has long pondered, reaching conclusions only after weighing all the possibilities. About himself, though, he's quite critical, a quality one might not expect from an important conductor. There are things he wishes he did better, like keeping a lid on his temper when things go wrong in rehearsal. He hopes to improve. He sees himself as a work in progress.

Clearly, this is a man of large gifts and amazing abilities, a man whose measure is not easily or quickly taken.

Michael Anthony

Coming to Minnesota

Eiji Oue would be leaving at the end of his seventh season
as music director of the Minnesota Orchestra.
A search committee began looking for his replacement.

The Tenth Music Director

The search committee of the Minnesota Orchestra, charged with finding a replacement for Eiji Oue, hoped to get a new music director named by the orchestra's centennial year, 2002-2003. The list of "possibles" kept growing, though there was a short list, too, and three names on that list were scheduled to appear as guest conductors during the 2000-2001 season—an Italian, Roberto Abbado; a Russian, Yakov Kreizberg; and Osmo Vänskä, a Finn—though who knew if any of the three would say yes should an offer be made? There was talk, too, of the erratic but brilliant Christoph Eschenbach, the former music director of the Houston Symphony who was then just starting as chief conductor of the Orchestre de Paris.

Of the first three, Abbado was perhaps the best known in the United States, though Vänskä's recordings of Sibelius with the Lahti Symphony Orchestra were being viewed with increasing esteem in this country, and his career was clearly on the upswing. Within the prior twelve months he had led the Lahti orchestra at Avery Fisher Hall in New York City and the BBC Scottish Symphony Orchestra, of which he was then chief conductor, on a United States tour. He had made his conducting debuts with the St. Louis Symphony Orchestra, the National Symphony Orchestra, and the Chicago Symphony Orchestra, receiving enthusiastic reviews for each. And he wasn't a complete stranger to the Twin Cities. In 1994, he had played clarinet in a concert at the University of Minnesota as part of a brief United States tour by a chamber ensemble from the Lahti orchestra. In addition, in March 2000, he had appeared as guest conductor with The Saint Paul Chamber Orchestra. Of the three possible guest conductors, Vänskä was offering by far the most novel program—all Finnish works including the premiere of a harp concerto by Einojuhani Rautavaara, the elder statesman of Finnish composers, and two works by Sibelius, the less-often-heard Symphony No. 6 and the Violin Concerto with Joshua Bell as soloist.

The interest of the search committee was high, therefore, the night of October 12, 2000, when the sandy-haired, bespectacled forty-eight-year-old Vänskä walked briskly to the podium of Orchestra Hall, took a quick bow to polite applause, and, with barely a pause, gestured to the cellos and basses on his right to begin the melancholy theme that initiates the Rautavaara concerto, a tune that rises slowly like a cloud of smoke, accompanied in the distance by a solo horn. The harp—the skillful principal harp of this orchestra, Kathy Kienzle—enters with a sly, tentative theme of its own, as if someone were carefully walking out onto a lake of ice. After suggestions of turbulence from the orchestra, the harp accompanies a lush melody in the solo cello, and the movement ends in thick dramatic chords from the harp. The middle of the three movements is dominated by a ruminative harp cadenza, and, in the more agitated finale, the solo part is punctuated by chimes, vibraharp, and an instrument called a flexatone which sounds like someone bowing a saw. The concerto made a strong impression. Rautavaara, who was present for the performance, joined the musicians for a bow and looked very pleased.

The evening continued from the sublime to the sublime with an uncommonly thoughtful collaboration between Vänskä and Joshua Bell in the Violin Concerto. Familiar as this work is, the performance on this occasion revealed colors and details that are usually only hinted (or raced through, as in the famous Jascha Heifetz recording). Partly it was the relaxed feeling of the opening movement, a matter of Vänskä's tempo—slightly slower than is customary—along with Bell's willingness to linger over certain details and harmonic shifts, at times simply letting the music float along effortlessly. The middle movement, too, seemed to evolve organically, as if it were being composed on the spot, the music taking on an emotional tone of undeniable yearning and regret. The finale was properly quick and vital but never taken so fast as to blur the rhythms. Obviously, this is music that Vänskä had lived with and thought about for much of his career. The same impression was created after intermission with the Symphony No. 6, Sibelius's most radiantly beautiful, perhaps most Mozartean score. In most readings the work moves slowly and smoothly, whereas Vänskä enforced taut rhythm and precise articulation, establishing a chamber music texture in which the woodwind lines were always prominent. Balances were carefully judged, and the finale emerged with impressive force.

Indeed, this was an energizing, thought-provoking concert, the kind of music-making that had become rare at Orchestra Hall. If Vänskä had set out to make a strong impression, he succeeded. And, as it turned out, the musicians were no less excited than the audience. Flutist Wendy Williams has especially vivid memories of Vänskä's debut. She was pregnant at the time. In fact, the last of the four con-certs that Vänskä conducted that week was the last concert she played before her baby was born. "I remember holding those sustained thirds of which Sibelius is so fond while all this wild kicking was going on inside me," she said. "I remember liking Osmo very much. I liked his whole approach. He's a woodwind player, and he has a lot of faith that the wind players will do their job. He sort of leaves us alone, more than he does the strings."

Violist Sam Bergman recalls that his mother came to visit that week and asked about the concert she was going to hear. She inquired about the conductor. He told her, "It's this Finnish guy, Osmo Vänskä." She asked how the concert was going to be. He said, "I have no idea, but the rehearsals have been good. He really works us hard. He does a lot of detail work, and there's always the question with detail conductors: When they get to the concert, are they going to be able to step back and let the energy come through, or are they going to micro-manage every little thing?" Well, he absolutely did step back. Sam recalled one of those detail moments. "Two brass players came together on a chord that wasn't quite in tune, the kind of thing you usually can't fix in a concert. But he fixed it. He just looked at them and went . . ." (He gestures, one finger up, one finger down.) "The chord tightened up immediately, and I thought, 'Wow! That took an incredible amount of self-awareness, to be able to do that in the middle of a concert and have it work.' And it didn't seem like he was showing up the musicians. The crowd couldn't see it." Afterward, Sam's mother, who hadn't heard the orchestra in a number of years, said, "Does this orchestra always sound like that?" "I said 'It never sounds like that. It always sounds good, but this is something different.' A lot of us backstage had been approaching the musicians who were members of the search committee, asking, 'Is he on the list?' And they said yes. I remember telling my mother, 'I have absolutely no basis for saying this, but I think it's possible that you just saw the next music director.'"

Kienzle adds a final point: "Osmo was such an unknown when he first conducted here. Most of us didn't even know he was being considered for music director." As former board chair Luella Goldberg recalls, "Suddenly, board members were talking about someone named Osmo Vänskä and about the way he had built the Lahti orchestra and brought it to worldwide attention."

Amid the growing enthusiasm for Vänskä that autumn, there were nay-sayers, too, but they weren't questioning Vänskä's musicianship or abilities. They were suggesting that one program is not enough to assess a conductor, that he should be re-engaged (which he already was, for the following season), and that he ought to be heard in a more conventional program.

Board chair Douglas Leatherdale argued the opposing view. "Had we waited, there was a good chance that he wouldn't be available the following year. I did push this thing," he said. "I felt we had to get on with the job, that we couldn't continue to procrastinate." Leatherdale interviewed Vänskä during the second and third periods of a hockey game at the Xcel Center in St. Paul. "Osmo was in line to get his picture taken with the Stanley Cup. He felt his friends back in Finland would be as impressed with that as anything he had done in the music world." They also talked at length in Massachusetts, after one of Vänskä's concerts with the BBC Scottish Symphony Orchestra. He was impressed not only by the glowing reviews Vänskä had received in the United States and Europe, but also by the fact that, in almost all cases, he had been asked back by the orchestras which he had guest conducted.

David Hyslop, then president of the Minnesota Orchestra Association and a member of the search committee, substantiated Leatherdale's fears that other orchestras were pursuing Vänskä. "Osmo did very well with the National Symphony Orchestra. They would have wanted him as principal guest conductor. The other thing is that Hans Vonk, the music director in St. Louis, was quite ill and, as a result, there was interest there in Osmo, either as principal guest conductor or music director."

Moreover, there had been other opportunities, at least for the members of the search committee, to see and hear Vänskä at work. Hyslop had heard him in San Francisco, and, before that, he and orchestra general manager Robert Neu heard him with The Saint Paul Chamber Orchestra, after which Hyslop and staff member Reid McLean took Vänskä to a basketball game. Said Hyslop, "But, in February of 2000, before Osmo had appeared here with either orchestra, Henry Fogel [then president of the Chicago Symphony Orchestra] called me and said, 'You've got to come down and hear Osmo.' Now that's a tough orchestra. They've seen and heard everybody. So I went down there, and the concert went very well. I spent some time with Osmo after that, and we started a relationship. As time went on, he got bigger and bigger, and all the reports on him were good. I talked to the agents and to Hugh Macdonald at the BBC Scottish Symphony Orchestra and to Tuomas Kinberg, the manager in Lahti. They raved about him. It came back to us: 'This is the real thing.' What we saw and heard in all these encounters was not only deep, deep knowledge and a very kind man, but also one with great leadership qualities."

In March 2001, members of the committee heard Vänskä conduct the BBC Scottish Symphony Orchestra at Symphony Hall in Boston. That same month Hyslop caught Vänskä and that orchestra in a different program in Troy, New York.

Michael Steinberg, a musicologist and a close observer of the orchestra, had also joined the growing pro-Vänskä faction, having heard the concerts with The Saint Paul Chamber Orchestra and the BBC Scottish Symphony Orchestra. He also knew and admired Vänskä's recordings for BIS, especially the Sibelius discs, which he found to be "deeply investigative." He

"What we saw and heard in all these encounters was not only deep, deep knowledge and a very kind man, but also one with great leadership qualities."

David Hyslop

was impressed, too, he said, with "the music director half" of the equation. "When he was here I saw the commanding way he ran rehearsals, and I also learned in conversations with him the sense he has for all the things—other than when he's on the box waving his arms around—all the things that make this complicated machinery of a modern symphony orchestra function. I was impressed with his lucid and not at all vainglorious sense of the importance of tours and recordings and all the various management functions. It all sounded like the emanation of a really mature artist and human being, and that was a pretty irresistible combination."

Jorja Fleezanis, the orchestra's concertmaster and a member of the search committee, found

herself thinking of James Levine during Vänskä's introductory rehearsals at Orchestra Hall. Levine, music director of the Boston Symphony Orchestra, had been a teacher during her school years. "His philosophy of music making is based on the same premise as Osmo's," she said. "They deliver it differently, because they're trained in different schools and are very different people. But they both use the score as their point of departure, the notion being that when a composer writes the nuances and dynamics and the tempo indications, those things have to be

Osmo with Concertmaster Jorja Fleezanis.

studied and considered very carefully without a lot of dilution of one's own personal take on it. When we had those first rehearsals, I thought, 'This is such a clean, organized way of running rehearsals, the result of which brought such clarity to the playing, I want to talk to this man. I really want to know who he is.'"

She invited him to join her at a nearby restaurant after one of the concerts just to get acquainted. "Sometimes meetings like that can be disappointing," she said. "The only thing I can say is that he was extremely what he was. There was nothing mysterious about him. He said he felt a strong reaction to the orchestra. He loved the willingness and the sort of hunger the orchestra has to play at a high level. It's a funny thing about Osmo. It's not as though he's asking us for something that's not there. This is a funny thing about music in general. If you go with the idea of what's there and you go to the highest level of what's expected, meaning that you play well rhythmically and with great integrity inside the tempo, then you don't play approximately. As soon as you play approximately, you have something very different going on. It becomes a watercolor instead of a strongly-etched print of Rembrandt. And the strength of that I felt right away when I spoke with him that night. He's a very strong-minded person. I asked him about Finland and what it's like to live there, and he wasn't casual with me at all. He was trying to be warm in the way that he was able to be in the early stage of getting to know me. I think he was actually very touched that I wanted to know more about him."

By the spring of 2001, the search committee was so focused on Vänskä that, according to Hyslop, the committee never got around to a serious discussion with Abbado, who at that time was also being looked at by The Saint Paul Chamber Orchestra to succeed Hugh Wolff as music director. As for Kreizberg, Hyslop had gone to Berlin and to Indianapolis to hear him.

Meanwhile, in Finland, Vänskä was contemplating the offer that he was by now certain the orchestra would make. Fate seemed to step in one day when he came upon a magazine interview with the Finnish conductor Paavo Berglund. Asked to compare American orchestras, Berglund said, "The Minnesota Orchestra is the most musical ensemble in the United States." Berglund's words had always carried special weight for Vänskä. "Paavo has been some kind of model for me, and I would even say some kind of idol as far as how to be a conductor," Vänskä said later. "He does his job without compromises, and he uses every bit of rehearsal time. He is a great conductor and a little bit underrated. But he doesn't want to be a star. Actually, he hates this kind of star culture we have now. He just wants to do music."

Back in Minneapolis, the vote for Vänskä on the thirteen-member search committee on March 26 wasn't unanimous, according to Hyslop, but it was enough to make a recommendation to the board. The next step was the writing of a contract and negotiations with Vänskä's management, Harrison Parrott, which included a meeting in London with Vänskä's manager, Lydia Connolly. The next day Hyslop, Connolly, and Robert Neu met with Vänskä in Lahti to finalize the deal. "When we got to Lahti, I looked around, and the deal finally made sense," Hyslop said. "Lahti looks like Minnesota." The contract then had to be approved by the executive committee of the board and finally by the board itself. According to Hyslop, one board member protested that the orchestra couldn't afford Vänskä, who was to receive $600,000 for the first year of his four-year contract. Said Hyslop, "Actually, when we hired him, of the top ten orchestras in the country, Osmo was the seventh or eighth best paid."

Some weeks earlier, in Finland, when he got word of the offer from the orchestra, Vänskä burst into tears.

On May 25, 2001, at 10:00 a.m., on stage at Orchestra Hall crowded with reporters, photographers, assorted staff and board members, and out-of-town guests, Douglas Leatherdale announced Osmo Vänskä as the tenth music director of the Minnesota Orchestra. Leatherdale spoke first, talking about "the two-year process that led us to Osmo Vänskä," adding that "under his artistic leadership, we feel the Minnesota Orchestra will continue to flourish as one of the world's top symphonies and one of the Twin Cities' premiere arts organizations." Hyslop, by way of introducing the conductor, spoke of his "superb artistic ability, thoughtful artistic vision, and inspirational musical personality."

Much of this was the standard rhetoric of such events. Vänskä, on the other hand, having flown in from Lahti the night before, seemed to be speaking from the heart when he said in a prepared statement, "I feel deeply happy and privileged to have been offered the position of music director of the Minnesota Orchestra, and to be on the threshold of a sustained period of outstanding music-making with these wonderful musicians. It is clear to me that Minnesota has all the qualities that make a truly great international symphony orchestra, and I am thrilled at the prospect of sharing and communicating our music vision through concerts, tours, and recordings. I have already been made to feel completely at home in Minnesota by the players, by the orchestra's superb management team, and by its board, and I very much look forward now to deepening my relationship in the coming seasons with the broader local community, whose support for the orchestra is so tremendously appreciated."

In the question period that followed, Vänskä proved to be droll and thoughtful. Asked why he took this position, he said, "Some orchestras had asked me the past few years to be principal conductor or principal guest. The offer here was much more serious. Also, the timing was right. And I can say that this was the best orchestra that asked. Of course, I had to think hard, and, actually, I had quite a long time to think, because I heard the first rumors about this almost two years ago. And after I had been here, it was quite clear to me, if the question came, that the answer would be yes. This is a great orchestra."

He was asked for his reaction to his first concerts here the previous October. "I felt very comfortable here," he said. "I felt that they enjoyed more and more when I worked them harder and harder. And I understood that this orchestra wants to do things better and better. They want to show what they can do, and this is ideal for a conductor."

Turning the focus to his native country, Vänskä was asked a question that has intrigued many: Why does Finland produce so many conductors and singers? Is it, as some say, because of good music education? "This is true," he said. "We have good music schools. I live in a small city, Riihimäki, 25,000 people. In one school we have a special music system. It goes for six years starting when the child is six or seven, and then there's choir and band. Also, there's the Music Institute, which is separate from the public schools, and these institutes are in every city. Then there are the conservatories. And it's cheap. The whole season for one child might be $35. That's one of the reasons I accept that we pay a lot of tax. The whole philosophy in the Nordic countries is that the state collects a lot of money, but they take care of your social security, your culture. The other reason for the health of our musical life is Sibelius. We got our independence in 1917. Before that we were under the power of the Russians. Sibelius was one of the first international persons in Finland. When the situation between the Finnish and the Russians was very tight, we had censorship of newspapers. Anything bad about the Russians was taken away. But when Sibelius wrote 'Finlandia' or the Second Symphony, everybody knew what he was saying, but the censor couldn't

do anything about it. I used to say if you go to Helsinki and ask ten people to name the ten most important names in Finnish history, I'm sure that eight or nine of them will say Sibelius. In which other country would that be true?"

Vänskä was asked whether he intended to program American music during his years here. "I don't know much about American music, but I intend to learn. We used to say if the Finnish orchestras don't play Finnish music, who will? It's the same here." Then he was asked about the concern of many orchestras with attracting new audiences, especially young people. Did he have any tricks or any new formats to attract those people? "No," he said. "We can't do special lighting or balloons. All we can do is play the best music we can in the best possible way. That's our goal."

Details of the contract were also revealed that day. Under the terms of an initial four-year contract, Vänskä would lead the orchestra in twelve subscription weeks a year, plus additional weeks for national and international touring and recording. He would also complete his six-year tenure with the BBC Scottish Symphony Orchestra at the close of the 2001-2002 season and would continue his association with the Lahti Symphony Orchestra. (He stepped down in 2008 and was named Conductor Laureate.) He would establish a home in Minneapolis.

In August 2002, Vänskä met with the board and presented his artistic vision for the orchestra, a scheme that included, during his inaugural season of 2003-2004, two bold ideas: a trip to Europe and the initiation of a record set of Beethoven symphonies, both of which would cost serious money. Hyslop recalled the meeting. "The stock market was dropping fairly dramatically at that time, and I could tell that some board members were getting tense. But Osmo was very up-front, saying this doesn't mean we can afford to do all these things, but I think we're positioned to do them, especially the recordings and the tour. I went to Leatherdale

"We can't do special lighting or balloons. All we can do is play the best music we can in the best possible way. That's our goal."

Osmo Vänskä

and said, 'I am going to talk to Kenneth Dayton and suggest that he do an artistic initiative fund. Ken did something like that for Edo de Waart, but most of the money got spent on deficits.' Doug said, 'Go for it.'"

Dayton and his wife, Judy, were long-time benefactors of the orchestra. Hyslop had lunch with Dayton on August 20, knowing that Dayton wasn't well. "I said to Ken, 'I know you're ill.' He said, 'I'm not ill. I'm dying.' I said 'I am not in favor of doing frivolous things, but we're positioned very well right now, and I know you believe in Vänskä. Would you consider doing the artistic initiative, which includes the tour of 2004 and the rest of it?' And this very sick guy grabbed my hand and, with tears in his eyes, he said, 'I'll talk to Judy, and we'll think about it.'"

"I was concerned that we had finally come to the point where the orchestra is playing like gangbusters and we've got a phenomenally gifted conductor," Hyslop said. "I didn't want to do what we did when the name was changed [the Minneapolis Symphony became the Minnesota Orchestra in 1968]: less touring and less recording at a time when people needed to know who we were. And now we bring in a superb conductor, and the first thing we tell him is, 'No more touring or recordings and no Carnegie Hall.' That's not a smart move, is it?"

On September 30, Hyslop sent Dayton a formal letter outlining a 2003-2008 initiative that would cost $4.3 million. In early December, Dayton sent Hyslop a response saying he and his wife would fund the first phase of the initiative with $1.6 million and judge the remaining requests in time. Eventually, other board members contributed to the fund.

Dayton, however, didn't live to see Vänskä step to the podium as music director. He died July 19, just two months before Vänskä's official opening night.

True to the Daytons' word, Judy Dayton has continued to fund a series of significant artistic initiatives—including touring and recording activity—that were to become hallmarks of Vänskä's tenure with the orchestra.

The Selling of Osmo

By the time Osmo made his official debut as music director, the night of September 11, 2003, some sixteen months after the press conference announcing his appointment, he was a known quantity in the Twin Cities. As music director designate, he had conducted the orchestra in five programs, interviewers had probed his psyche and pontificated on Finnish national culture, and the musicians had talked repeatedly of their admiration for their new conductor.

Even so, there had been occasional revelations during this interim period—confirmations, already known to anyone familiar with the conductor's many recordings, that his expertise as far as repertoire extended a good deal beyond Sibelius. There was, for instance, the memorable, cold night in January 2003, when the program included the premiere of a work by the British composer Judith Weir, "The welcome arrival of rain," a beguiling piece abounding in aural images of nature and subtle Eastern-style percussion effects, all attentively played. In turn, the Jacques Ibert Flute Concerto, with Emmanuel Pahud as soloist, proceeded in proper French style

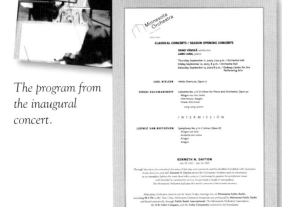

The program from the inaugural concert.

with a light touch and delicate, fine-spun string playing. The finale, Sergei Rachmaninoff's Symphony No. 2, turned up the heat a good deal. This was a study in carefully-controlled passion, warm-toned, high in contrast, the lyrical passages smooth and flowing, and the bigger rhetorical, martial moments surging with energy. Already this was sounding like a different orchestra. The playing showed a precision and rhythmic certainty that had not been heard here in years.

A week earlier, Osmo had collaborated with the Russian violinist Viktoria Mullova in a powerful reading of the Bela Bartók Violin Concerto No. 2, a work this orchestra recorded in the 1950s with Yehudi Menuhin. More so than the recording, this was a riveting performance of such commitment and intensity that even the third movement, which can seem disjointed, flowed effortlessly and logically. Mullova easily managed the work's pyrotechnics, and both violinist and conductor, showing special rapport, gave an unerring account of the music's alternating tension and repose. One other concerto performance of that season was memorable: Aram Khachaturian's gaudy neo-nineteenth-century piano concerto played by Jean-Yves Thibaudet. This is a work that in a really good performance can almost manage to sound second rate. Thibaudet, with Osmo's astute help, brought it up to the mark, playing with fierce energy and momentum. For sheer daredevil virtuosity, this was the performance of the season.

Vänskä's inaugural program as music director in September 2003 managed both to look toward the immediate future and to indulge in a burst of fireworks, the latter provided by the young Chinese pianist Lang Lang, who played Rachmaninoff's Piano Concerto No. 3. The foreshadowing came in the curtain-raiser, Nielsen's "Helios" Overture, and in the evening's finale, Beethoven's Symphony No. 5. Nielsen's overture served as a prologue to the performance of all six of this composer's symphonies that Osmo had planned for his first two seasons. Nielsen, painting a sonic portrait of the sun's journey from dawn to sunset over the Aegean Sea, made a bright, sonorous curtain-raiser. But it was the Beethoven symphony, the first in the set of Beethoven symphonies that the orchestra would begin recording later in the season, that dominated the evening. Here was a compelling performance with the kind of close attention to the score, along with shrewdly judged tempos—very close to Beethoven's controversial metronome timings—that are not often heard. The outer movements bristled with energy and restlessness, while the build-up of tension going into the finale was an edge-of-the-seat experience. The opening of the scherzo was perfect: soft and fast in a way that hardly any other conductor does it, even though that's what Beethoven asked for, and, in a surprising gesture, there was no slowing down for the trio. Lang's Rachmaninoff offered moments of excitement, too, though less insight.

For the audience and the musicians—and for Osmo, too—the concert was an auspicious start of a new era in the orchestra's history. For the orchestra's public relations department, Osmo's debut concert was the end of a long campaign aimed at introducing the new conductor to the community, the culmination of sixteen months of planning meetings and head-scratching and brain-storming by an inaugural committee, all centering on a promotion that would be high in impact and yet would still convey the message that the new guy at the podium is a serious conductor and worthy of respect.

To increase ticket sales, the staff knew they had to do something—and something that Osmo would accept. One idea was a pair of free concerts right after Osmo's subscription debut, one at the Lake Harriet Bandshell and another under the sponsorship of Target stores at Peavey Plaza, adjacent to Orchestra Hall. For this "Picnic with Osmo," the plaza would be transformed into a picnic ground with a giant carpet of grass covering the audience-seating area. Gwen Pappas, the orchestra's director of public relations, said, "Target would promote the heck out of it and would run a full-page ad for the event. The ad was a graphic of Osmo in shorts and sunglasses waving a turkey drumstick over his head as if it were his baton. The idea was 'Come on down and meet the new music director of the orchestra.' It was vintage Target: fresh and out-of-the-box. Everyone in the organization liked it and felt that, if Osmo was OK with it, we would run it. So we e-mailed the graphic to Osmo and held our breath. I mean, the thing did look like

he was in his underwear. Well, he got back to us and said it was fine and added, 'I think we take ourselves too seriously.' So that was for us the first indication that musically he's very serious, but he's also OK with a more playful image."

Then there was the Osmo doll, a six-inch bobble-arm figure in Osmo's image, more or less, in concert garb with a baton in his hand. Designed and built by Target, the dolls were used as promotion for season subscriptions and special events as a give-away and were never actually offered for sale. Several thousand were made. In this case, too, Osmo had to approve the idea. "The problem was that Osmo didn't know what a bobble-head doll was," said Pappas. "We had to explain it. We said, 'Well, usually, the head bobs, but in this case, the arm's going to bob.' And he just accepted it. He was game to give it a try."

She notes that in later months and seasons Osmo was less accepting of certain marketing and public relations efforts that promoted him over the orchestra. Said Pappas, "He has actually called the marketing department and said, 'It shouldn't be only my name in these titles. It should be me *and* the orchestra.'"

Osmo weighed in on the subject. "I hate to hear on the radio when the announcer says, 'Maestro so-and-so conducted the Berlioz *Symphonie fantastique*' with not a word about the orchestra. That's wrong. But it's also wrong if they say, 'The National Orchestra of France played the *Symphonie fantastique*.' It must be both—the orchestra and the conductor. Karajan, for instance, was one of the superstars. They would say, 'Karajan's Fifth Symphony.' No. It's Beethoven's Fifth Symphony. For me, that's a red flag. I hate that. Whereas, in an ideal case—and I think that happened in Lahti—we become like a trademark, and I hope that happens here. If someone speaks of the Minnesota Orchestra, they know that Vänskä is the conductor. If someone speaks about Vänskä, they know that it's the Minnesota Orchestra. They belong together."

In 2005, Osmo's image, a photograph about twenty feet high, was placed permanently on the front of Orchestra Hall. Osmo didn't like it at first. "But then Gwen and others motivated me. I mean, I know that a conductor's face, especially in America, is some kind of huge and important market tool. So with that in mind, I began to accept it."

Beyond that, he admits to being uneasy about the concept of the conductor as star. It's what his manager, Lydia Connolly, calls "the fame thing." "Being music director of an American orchestra involves responsibilities that you don't necessarily get in Europe," Connolly said.

"I know it's part of the business," said Osmo. "But still I feel sometimes uncomfortable with it. We all are doing the music together. I think of it this way: Say there are two concerts. One is the conductor without the orchestra. The other is the orchestra without the conductor. I prefer the second one. But we need each other."

As it happens, the identification of conductor and orchestra seems to be solidifying. According to marketing figures, attendance at Orchestra Hall rises when Osmo is conducting as opposed to when a guest is at the podium. Ticket sales in general, but especially single ticket sales, have slowly risen during the Vänskä years. "But it's not as though we're playing to ninety-five percent capacity," said Pappas. (By early 2009, over-all attendance at Orchestra Hall stood at seventy-two percent of capacity.) "I think the wisdom now is that there is no silver bullet, no particular music director or guest artist or program that, over the long haul, is going to elevate those numbers in a significant way. Instead, it's going to be a gradual process of building trust, inviting new people in and building trust in them and letting them choose whatever kind of concerts they want to attend."

"I would like to concentrate
on the music—music that
we can play with the
highest possible level of quality,
but also with heart. . . .
We can go beyond the notes
and give people of the audience
a real experience,
a touch for things which are
bigger than life."

Osmo Vänskä

With Finnish Roots

It has come to be called "the Finnish miracle,"
the startling number of conductors who have emerged in recent decades
from the Sibelius Academy, and in many cases have established international careers.

The Finnish Context

We like to think we know the Finns—those hardy, perhaps slightly masochistic people who beat each other with birch sticks in their saunas and who embody the notion of *sisu*, which means "guts," suggesting courage, stubbornness, stamina, and a fierce determination to do what needs to be done. The young people of Finland out-distance the rest of the world in the specialized art of air guitar—strumming a non-existing guitar to a backing track. Older Finns are enraptured with tango dancing, not the sensual Argentine variety, but what Morley Safer once described as "a sad shuffle in a minor key."

The Finns are full of contradictions. Richard D. Lewis, author of *Finland: Cultural Lone Wolf*, lists a few of them: "Finns are warm-hearted, but they seek solitude. They are hard-working and intelligent but often slow to react. They love freedom, but they curtail their own liberty by closing their shops early, limiting their access to alcohol, and taxing themselves to death. They are fiercely individualistic but are afraid of 'what the neighbors might say.'"

What many people most admire from afar about this tiny country of just over five million people is that here is a social democracy that really works for the betterment of its citizens, a country whose education level is the highest in Europe, and whose government in the early 1970s began devoting a large part of its tax revenue to financing music education and providing subsidies to composers and performers. The result is a network of 150 academies, thirty-one orchestras, eleven regional opera companies, and forty-five annual festivals attended by flocks of eager, informed concertgoers. Add to that what has come to be called "the Finnish miracle," the startling number of conductors who have emerged in recent decades from Helsinki's Sibelius Academy and in many cases have established international careers: Esa-Pekka Salonen, Jukka-Pekka Saraste, Okko Kamu, Mikko Franck, Susanna Malkki, Eri Klas, Sakari Oramo, and Osmo Vänskä. An earlier generation would include names such as Leif Segerstam, Ulf Söderblom, and Tauno Hannikainen, along with the father of them all, Robert Kajanus.

"Composers are celebrated in Finland," says Marjo Heiskanen, of the Finnish Music Information Center in Helsinki, an organization devoted to the promotion of Finnish music both at home and around the world. Heiskanen, herself a composer who began writing music in the 1980s, is the organization's director of contemporary music.

"Currently there are about 100 professional composers in Finland," she said. "Most of them have a grant going on at any time of the year. Others have teaching jobs at various institutes or at the Sibelius Academy. And some are working musicians. Any musician in Finland can make a living, either composing or playing."

Osmo Vänskä is one of those working musicians.

Growing Up in Finland

Osmo's mother, Maire Toivanen Vänskä, lives in a cheerful three-room condominium in Kotka. It is infused with memories. Shelves of photos—old and new—fill a display case along a living room wall, sharing space with gifts and memorabilia, signs of a long, well-spent, well-connected, busy life. A widow since 1988 when her husband Yrjö died of heart failure, Maire seems a bit fragile at eighty-eight, though it's clear that her life has been a testament of strength, endurance, and the sustaining love of family, a consolation that continues to the present time. She endured the hardships of World War II and the ensuing decade of almost constant moving from town to town, of finally settling in this city of Kotka and running a produce store with her husband while raising a family of three sons—one of whom became a missionary, one a pastor, and a third, the youngest, evolving into a world-famous conductor. She now has twelve grandchildren and nine great-grandchildren.

Osmo's mother Maire and father Yrjö Vänskä.

If the theme of her life up until recent years was work, Maire shows no bitterness in recalling it. For her, work was simply a matter of doing what had to be done. "We learned to work in our own poor home where I was one of seven sons and three daughters," she says. Born in Kurkijoki in the central part of Finnish Karelia in 1920, she has a photograph of a painting one of her brothers had done many years ago: a wooden cottage with ten children scattered near the doorway—the cottage where Maire was born. "It was two rooms for thirteen people," she said. (A grandmother lived with the parents and children.) "We children walked five kilometers to and from school." As a teenager, she worked as a clerk in a cooperative store in Elisenvaara, and it was there that she met Yrjö, a shoemaker from nearby Parikkala. They were married in Elisenvaara on May 29, 1939.

Six months later, on November 30, the newlyweds' lives and the lives of all Finns were thrown into upheaval when the Soviet Union attacked its little neighbor to the west with the expectation that Finland would be defeated within two to four weeks. But the country united against the aggressor, and the Soviets were routed in several key battles. By March 1940, sheer exhaustion led to a peace treaty. The Finnish army was running out of even the most basic material, and the Soviet Union wanted to end the costly war that had become an international embarrassment. Finland was the loser in the treaty and had to make significant territorial concessions. With the Moscow Peace, some 400,000 Finns, one-tenth of the population, were ordered out of eastern Finland, which had been given to the Soviets.

Yrjö went into the military. Raimo, the eldest son and now a retired pastor, picks up the story: "Mother walked fifteen kilometers to her home, where her parents lived. There they were told they had to leave the following day at 1:00 p.m. They had to be on the train with only the luggage they could carry. Mother's brothers drove the cattle to the Finnish side. When he could, Father came from the frontier to help."

Eventually Yrjö was able to stay home, finding work on the railway coming from Tampere, and the couple settled in Lahti, where Raimo was born in 1941. (A first son, born a year earlier, died after five weeks.) Raimo said, "When the cease fire came in 1944, the Finnish soldiers collected their guns and materials and walked to Lahti. They left their guns there and started civilian life. So I think today when the Lahti Symphony Orchestra puts up those big banners inviting people to come to a concert, if Papa had seen this, it would have been a special thing for him, because he had seen all the misery of the war and the losses."

The family moved often in the years after the war, as did many Finns, and the family gradually grew as well. Raimo provides a chronology of towns: Lahti, Parikkala, Savitaipale (where Seppo was born in 1947), Hyvinkää, Orivesi, Simpele, Savonlinna (where Osmo Antero was born in 1953), and on to Aura, Lohja, Karkkila and, home at last, Kotka in 1957, where all three sons were eventually married: Raimo in 1965, Seppo in 1970, and Osmo in 1973. Maire and Yrjö set up a grocery store behind their house. "All those earlier moves were hard for Raimo," Osmo recalled later. "He had to change city and school sometimes three times in one year. That's hard for kids, whereas I was able to grow up mostly in one place."

Both parents worked every day in the store. "My parents' generation was really hard-working," Osmo said. "There were long days, but they didn't complain." He sees this as partly a reaction to their war experiences and the difficult years immediately after. "It was really a question of survival," he

said. "They had to start a new life, and you don't complain about your situation. You just work harder. But I will say they took really good care of us. Our home was always clean. Our clothes were maybe not new but always washed and ironed. My mom made great food, and it all had to be prepared. At that time you didn't think about how much time that takes. I mean, she would work ten hours in the store, then start all her work at home. Looking back on it today, I don't understand how that was possible."

Yrjö was a small, intense, wiry man, a man who has known hard times. In gatherings with his family, though, he looks relaxed and happy. "He wasn't tough, but he wasn't easy, either," Osmo recalled. "He knew the rules, and he expected us to follow them. But he wasn't some kind of controller who was always behind you. So there was discipline for the three kids. What I have learned since is that my mother had a very strong will, though at the time I didn't see that she was using that will. I think that I have gotten many characteristics from my mother, like the

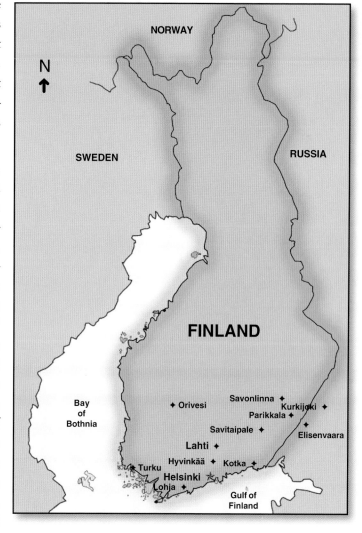

notion that if you have to do something, do it as well as you can. But that came from my father, too."

The older boys helped out in the store, though the parents didn't demand it. As he got older, Osmo acted as delivery boy, riding his bike around town. "They didn't pay me much, but I got so many sodas to drink that I was quite expensive—and some nice cakes, too."

Missionary brother Seppo writes from Japan: "Osmo was mostly in a good mood as a child, a smiling, nice fellow. He was loved by all the older ladies in our neighborhood and the church." Raimo, too, says that Osmo was the favorite in the family and in the neighborhood.

Maire is more diplomatic. "I loved them all in the same manner, and every one of them was a credit," she says. Pressed on the point, she admits that "Osmo was the beloved one for the mother. He was so courageous and open-minded." She recalls that as a kid he once jumped up into the cabin of a truck that was parked at a trucking company near their house, and there she saw him, seated next to the driver. "He wanted to go to Helsinki," she said. "He was eager for new ideas and experiences." "I actually remember this," said Osmo later. "I got in this red truck. I was maybe five or six. It was my dream to get to Helsinki. With my moth-

Osmo and brother Seppo in earlier times.

er's permission we aranged for me to go along with a driver to Helsinki. We had to deliver things from Kotka to Helsinki and then reload and come back to Kotka. This was about ninety-five miles, but in those days it was a full day's trip, and I was so happy to do it."

Anyone who knew the Vänskäs at that time wouldn't have been surprised that Osmo started violin lessons at the age of nine. This was a musical family. As a young man Yrjö had played violin in a dance band, and the next generation kept the music playing. Raimo, too, played violin, and Seppo studied trumpet.

And, as Seppo recalled, this family of devout Lutherans often sang hymns together at home. "And we all went to music school two or three times a week," he said. Music has continued down the family tree. Among Seppo's children, the oldest, Simo, plays trombone, and the two youngest daughters play violin. Elina, the second oldest, is a flute teacher, and Satu, born in 1979, is a violinist with the Australian Chamber Orchestra.

An Instrument of My Own

Osmo took most of his violin lessons at the home of his teacher, Jukka Lahdenkyla, who lived not far from the Vänskä house. Other times the lessons were at the Kotka Music Institute. He found the violin difficult, but it was clear to him even at that young age that a whole world was opening up to him. "I loved this idea of being able to play, of having my own instrument," he said. "But the clarinet was easier for me." He got his first clarinet a year after he started violin lessons, when his church had started a wind ensemble. They gave Seppo a trumpet and Osmo a clarinet. "No one asked me what I wanted to play. I just got this clarinet," he said. "It was an old instrument someone had donated. The band was forty players. Almost everyone in the band was starting from zero. The oldest players were fourteen or fifteen. The program at the church was that those who played in the band also got private lessons."

At age ten, Osmo had found his instrument, and then, through the church, he found the man who would be his teacher for the next six years, Terho Koljonen. "He was very proper and always wore a bow tie," Osmo recalled. "He was in the military band, and he played in the German system, which was quite rare then in Finland, where it was usually the French system. The fingering is different. Koljonen was a good teacher for me because I always want to go fast. I have never been a great one to practice, but I was lucky—I learned quickly. And when you're nine or ten, the playing is really like playing. It's not like work. And, of course, when it's the last minute, right before the lesson, you work really fast. And I was happy that almost right away I was able to play music with other kids. The Music Institute organized some chamber music. We played duos and trios, and sometimes five or six played. The idea of playing together has always been important to me."

At age thirteen, Osmo reached a crossroad. Two things had become clear. One was that he had real talent as a musician. The other was that, if he wanted to become a professional player, he would eventually have to attend the Sibelius Academy in Helsinki, where the best teachers were. The shortest route to that goal involved changing schools, going from a four-year high school program to one that took just two years. This meant less of an all-round education but more musical training, not just clarinet lessons but musical history and theory. By following this plan in just two years he could join the military band in Helsinki, which would give him entrée to the Sibelius Academy. Music, it seemed, had taken over his life, which meant that his other studies—geography, history, for example—were suffering.

"Osmo was even worse in school than I was in those early days," said Seppo. All this involved more than a few high-level family conferences, given that the aspiring musician couldn't change schools without his parents' permission. Maire remembered those conferences. "Leaving the regular school was discussed," she said. "But we felt it was Osmo's decision. He went his own path."

Osmo knew there was some risk involved. For one thing, there weren't all that many openings for a professional clarinetist in a small country like Finland. "It was like a card game," he said. "I put everything on one card. What would have happened if I couldn't play well enough? What if I couldn't get a job as a clarinetist? Instead of getting a normal education, I knew that I wanted to play, and so I went as quickly as possible for that. And in my case, it

worked. I have been able to get more education later on. But I can see also the other side. What if I hadn't been able to make it? I have thought about this. Maybe I wanted it so much because I knew somewhere inside my soul or brain that I could do it."

A Professional Musician

His intuitions paid off. Osmo's next two teachers—Arvo Kuikka in the military band and Sven Lavela at the Sibelius Academy—produced a polished, albeit very young, professional musician; so polished that in 1971, at the age of 18, Osmo landed one of the best jobs a clarinetist can get in Finland: principal clarinet of the Turku Philharmonic Orchestra, the nation's oldest orchestra. The audition was blind, that is, behind a screen, and the screen wasn't removed until the winner was announced. Recalling that moment, Osmo laughed, "And there I was, this young guy. They were surprised."

At age ten, Osmo had found his instrument.

Lavela, with whom he was studying at the time, told him to take the job. "He didn't want to hold me back," Osmo said. But that meant he could not finish his studies with Lavela and therefore didn't get his diploma. During his first months in Turku he tried to keep up his lessons, making the two-hour drive to Helsinki once a week to work with his teacher. But then he gave up. "I got the job too early," Osmo said. "I'm not complaining. It was good for me. But when you are principal clarinet on that scale, with a relatively good orchestra, and you're playing concerts and chamber music and you're invited to do solo things, and then you're even invited to be a teacher, with all that, where is the time to complete your studies?"

And surprisingly, this eighteen year old got no static from his fellow musicians, many of whom were two and three times his age. "I was a good player at that time," he said. "I really earned my place there. For me it was easy to do the orchestra parts, and they liked what I was doing. I shouldn't be the person to say this, but I was some kind of a star in the orchestra. The older guys never gave me trouble."

In 1974, Osmo spent a few weeks in Berlin studying with Karl Leister, the famed principal clarinet of the Berlin Philharmonic, initiating what he later described as "a really important time in my life." For one thing, Leister taught a different style of playing—lighter and using less force than that to which Osmo was accustomed. The mouthpiece on Osmo's clarinet had fallen apart the week before he arrived in Berlin, and the substitute he got didn't fit him very well. Leister secured the services of a mouthpiece maker who was a player in the Deutsche Oper. He came to one of Osmo's lessons with Leister and there he fitted a new mouthpiece which, it turned out, never worked very well for Osmo. "But I learned many things from Leister," Osmo said. "I just needed some time to fix my breathing and my playing technique, and I was able to add something new to my playing. But, as happens so often in life, the learning came about in spite of an accident." Osmo and Leister have remained friends. Leister was the soloist on Osmo's first disc for BIS, a set of clarinet concertos by Bernhard Henrik Crusell. While in Berlin, Osmo was inspired by great performances of orchestras like the Berlin Philharmonic. He went to Berlin as a clarinet player and left with ideas about becoming a conductor.

The desire to conduct dates back to a boyhood day in the mid-1960s, Mother's Day to be exact, when the Vänskäs

Osmo with his father.

bought their first stereo set. The first record they bought was the Columbia LP of Leonard Bernstein conducting the New York Philharmonic in Brahms' Symphony No. 2, a work that was to play a role at significant points in his career. Osmo remembers this vividly. His sister-in-law Marjatta remembers seeing Osmo at twelve or thirteen standing in front of the phonograph conducting an imaginary orchestra with knitting needles in his hands. "The thing is," he said, "when I got my clarinet, it was obvious quite soon my dream was to be a professional clarinetist, even though I didn't know if I would be good enough to do it. But then a few years later, when I was listening to this record of Brahms, I had another dream: that it would be great to be a conductor. I have had these two dreams in my life: to be a clarinet player and to be a conductor. I have been lucky. I realized both dreams."

For a time the second dream lay quietly. Even so, Osmo paid close attention to the conductors he worked with in Turku, as he did during his later years in Helsinki. "I was always noticing what the conductor was doing and how well he was doing it. And even before that," he said, "at the summer music camps—I was maybe fourteen, fifteen—we had these young guys conducting the orchestra: Leif Segerstam, Okko Kamu. They were in their twenties, but they were great conductors, and I got inspiration from them.

"There were maybe 200 kids playing instruments in the summer music camp or Finnish Obisto. It was in a small village outside of Tampere, and they had a choir there, with another 150 or so. It's still operating. A lot of those kids with whom I played at those camps are now playing in professional orchestras or are teachers. That experience was very important for me. I had only a B-flat clarinet, as did most of the kids. I remember we were to play Brahms' Second Symphony. With B-flat clarinet, you have to play a half-step lower than what is written. And I had to transpose in a small room upstairs—very hot, no air-conditioning. It was hard, but it was so great to play in that orchestra. So I was really happy to play clarinet, and I never felt that this was not enough. But somewhere there was this idea that I would like to try conducting."

Opportunities arose. On arrival in Turku, Osmo had been asked to teach part-time at the local conservatory, which he did from 1971 to 1975. During his second year there, the director of the conservatory, Tuomas Haapanen, who later became a violin professor at the Sibelius Academy, said that he was too busy to conduct the school's chamber orchestra. Osmo volunteered to take over. He recalled that moment vividly. "I said, almost stuttering in my eagerness, 'Could I try it?' That was my first time with a chamber orchestra."

By then, he was also conducting a student choir in the town, a gospel ensemble connected to the Campus Crusade for Christ. Osmo calls this his first conducting experience.

Love and Marriage

One of the singers in the choir was an eighteen-year-old nursing student, Pirkko Penttinen, who had grown up in Juupajoki, a small town near Tempere, the fourth largest city in Finland. The daughter of a bank president and one of six children, Pirkko had dreamed of becoming an actress and living in Helsinki. But her parents convinced her that nursing was a more reliable pursuit. Her family had always been musical—her parents met in the church choir—and so it was natural that she continue singing as an avocation. She took notice of Osmo, and he of her. "She was different from the others, and that made her interesting," Osmo said.

Pirkko recalled their first meeting. The guy she was actually attracted to was Osmo's friend, Hannu Nyman, whom she had met at a school social on a Saturday night. They arranged for a later meeting, and he asked if he could bring his friend Osmo. What she first noticed were Osmo's shoes.

"I always look at shoes when I see people," she said. "His were grey suede. Actually, he was a stylish guy and a very nice person, but I was still thinking more of the other guy." They didn't meet again for eighteen months. "My roommate kind of opened my eyes. 'That Osmo, he's such a nice guy,' she said. 'That's true,' I said. 'Everybody likes him, but there's really nothing between us. I don't know. Maybe there is something, and we'll have to find out. And it turned out that he had the same feeling. 'OK,' he said, 'let's go driving after a rehearsal. We have to find out if there is something between us.' There was."

Just for the record, his view of the drive is the reverse: they went for a drive in order to prove to each other that there *wasn't* something between them.

While playing with the Turku Orchestra, Osmo (holding the score) directed a gospel choir, his first conducting experience.

She and Osmo didn't actually begin dating until eighteen months later, and six months after that they decided to get married. In July 1973, they went to visit Pirkko's mother, saying they would like to make plans for a wedding in August. As Osmo remembers it, she groaned. "Oh," she said, "I was just thinking that my summer would not be so busy and so difficult. And now you tell me this." Seppo had encouraged them to marry. "We had been wondering if we should wait," Osmo said. "But then Seppo gave a practical answer. He said, 'Hey, if you know that you love each other, if you know you would like to get married, do it! Why pay for two apartments? You can save money.' I am thankful to Seppo for saying this."

Was there any resistance from Pirkko's parents? Was there risk in marrying a musician? Pirkko says her parents never said anything negative. "But I know they were concerned," she added. "They never gave me a hard time," Osmo said. "They didn't do an investigation of me. Maybe they asked some questions about my job and what kind of salary I had. But I never felt that I wasn't welcome." He acknowledges, though, that a musician's life can be unstable, or at least is perceived that way by some people. "It's like the old joke," he said. "Two mothers are talking about their children. One asks, 'What is your child doing?' The other one responds, 'He's a musician.' The first one says, 'Yes, my son is an alcoholic, too.'"

Osmo's older brother Raimo presided at the marriage ceremony in 1973.

In 1977, Osmo took two important steps. He auditioned for and won the position of co-principal clarinet at the Helsinki Philharmonic Orchestra. The position at the Helsinki Philharmonic was the most important job for a clarinetist in Finland.

But the conducting dream wouldn't fade away. "When I was playing or listening to music," he said, "I was always thinking about whether the ensemble was together or how well they were playing. I think I used my ears not only to be aware of my own part, but also to hear how the whole system was going, and then how to fix it if it needed fixing." Besides, his prior conducting experiences, admittedly limited, had gone well.

"I was picking berries," Pirkko said. "Osmo came up to me and said he would like to go to the Sibelius Academy to be a conductor. I said, 'Oh, really?' But I never said no. It was only later, when he was a conductor and wanted to do that full-time, that I said, 'Oh, my God, I married a clarinetist. Who is this guy? I now have to call him a conductor.' But it's OK. I'm happy the way things turned out." She admits, though, that it was scary for a while because they would lose the income from Osmo's steady job with the Helsinki Philharmonic.

He started conducting studies at the Sibelius Academy. There was risk in this, not unlike the risk Osmo took at thirteen when he dropped out of the regular high school in Kotka. Only a few students were accepted each year in the conducting class—four or five—chiefly because there was only one main teacher at that time at the Academy, the formidable Jorma Panula. Osmo applied in the summer and was accepted along with three others. One of those, the late Esko Linnavalli, went on to form Finland's first professional jazz big band. The other two, Esa-Pekka Salonen and Jukka-Pekka Saraste, became world-famous conductors. Osmo was becoming a student again while maintaining his position with the orchestra.

Moreover, he was now a father. His first child, Tytti, had been born a year earlier.

Osmo's nephew, Simo, a mathematician who lives in Lahti, said that what he remembers most about Osmo is how hard he works—and not just at the podium. He recalled as a teenager visiting Osmo and Pirkko at their home in Rihiimäki. "Osmo was working in the garden, moving big, heavy rocks. I began to help," he said, "and I noticed that he was moving seven or eight rocks for every four or five I carried. He was almost running. The thing about him is that he's busy, but he always has time for you. And though he has become famous, he is still Uncle Osmo."

Osmo, his mother Maire, and brother Raimo.

Learning to Be a Conductor

Osmo spent two years (1977-1979) under Jorma Panula's tutelage, emerging from the academy with a conductor's degree, rather than an official diploma. (There was extra course work he didn't finish.) In countless interviews over the years, Osmo has questioned Panula's teaching methods and to a certain extent even Panula himself, who appears to have cultivated an image of eccentricity or, one might say, of eccentric brilliance. But Osmo's attitude toward his famous teacher is more complicated and ambivalent than has been reported and is worth examining in closer detail, partly because of Panula's eminence—he is surely the most important teacher of conducting in Europe—and partly for what it suggests about Osmo's own thoughts on conducting and the training of conductors.

Born in Finland in 1930, Panula served as chief conductor of the Turku Philharmonic Orchestra from 1963 to 1965 and the Helsinki Philharmonic Orchestra from 1965 to 1972. He was professor of conducting at the Sibelius Academy from 1973 to 1994. He has held teaching positions at important conservatories in several Nordic countries; he has taught master classes throughout Europe and, in one instance, in the U.S. He still teaches part-time at the Sibelius Academy. He is credited with two innovations in the training of conductors: the use of video and making available a full student orchestra on which a conductor may practice, rather than, as had been and still often is the case in conservatories, a piano.

One of Osmo's classmates, Saraste, when asked what Panula's strengths are as a teacher, said, "He's an enigma. He has learned some way of secretly guiding one's personality, and the student has to be quite responsive to this. Panula doesn't offer theories, and to be successful with him one has to counter that lack of theory." Saraste spent three years with Panula. "The first thing I learned: to economize your messages," he said. "It's easy to capture the attention of twenty players in a chamber orchestra but not so easy with a hundred. The feedback with twenty is direct, whereas with a hundred you have to manage the feedback."

Vesa Sirén, music critic of the *Helsingin Sanomat*, the daily newspaper in Helsinki, has often observed Panula in the classroom. Panula's method, he said, was influenced by Eastern philosophy. "First, he doesn't teach you against your will; second, you must ask, you must be curious, you must find out. In other words, he's not lecturing. He said to me once, 'In a perfect system, I wouldn't say anything. They would conduct, watch the videos, see how horrible they are, and then adjust.' The things that he kept repeating in the classes that I attended were, 'Don't do too much. They are playing. Don't bother them.' Another idea of his: Phrasing is more important than technique. And he's good at identifying students' mannerisms. Panula's methods are not very polite, but they can be effective." Sirén said there is no ill will on Panula's part toward Osmo. "It's just that they were a little distant. He didn't get to know him as well as he did Esa-Pekka [Salonen] and Jukka-Pekka [Saraste]."

Osmo said he admired Panula for his innovative use of video and a full orchestra. "When you see yourself on video, you can learn so much. And you get so embarrassed when you see those tapes."

In one of the interviews, Osmo was asked to say something about Panula's "speaking hands."

Osmo: His idea is that a conductor shouldn't speak but use his hands to tell everything that an orchestra needs to know. But, of course, you can't only do that. You have to be able to communicate your ideas.

There was a time when I think I was his favorite clarinet player. He often selected me to play with him on recordings.

Osmo became co-principal clarinet of the Helsinki Philharmonic Orchestra.

He's obviously smart and a fast worker, and you start to like him. He has brilliant musical ideas. But eventually I got tired of his idea of no responsibilities. His motto was "Do whatever you like." Yes, but I go to school to get a teacher who will tell me at least some of the time what to do. Why would I go to school if the only lesson is: Do whatever you like, and do it your way?

But I don't want to be too negative. There are points that I respect. But there are also a lot of disappointments and frustrations. And I'm not speaking only as a conductor but as a musician. When orchestra musicians are rehearsing, they need to repeat a few things several times. If they are not allowed to repeat or they just play the whole piece once through, then something is wrong. His motivation, he always said, was that they are professionals, so they don't need this.

A typical situation with him is that he says something and people say, "Wow!" No one actually understands what he said, but the atmosphere is that if you have to ask, then you look foolish. This is my dilemma about Panula. As I said, I was his clarinet player, and I think at that time he believed in me. But then I started to see these other things. I've thought about this so many times. I don't see how he can be a guru and doing master classes because, practically speaking, he doesn't say anything, unless it's something like, "Don't shake your hands so much."

Still, I know that some really good conductors have come from his classes. And I don't know if it was because that was the place where everyone went, and if you get everyone, then you get the best talents, too. My question is, and I don't have an answer, if we have Esa-Pekka [Salonen], Jukka-Pekka [Saraste], Sakari Oramo, or myself, what would

Jorma Panula

be different if we never went to this class? At that time, if any Finnish orchestra needed a young conductor to do school concerts or rehearsals or whatever, they always called Panula. You didn't get those concerts if you weren't in his class.

You spent only two years with him. Did you leave early?

Osmo: No, after my first year in the class, Panula suggested that I skip the second year and go right on to the third year. So I left after two years there. I don't know if it was that he wanted to put me away. Even if he did, I think he believed in me very much. He said, "You can start your career. You are strong enough to do that."

Do you think your time with Panula was wasted?

Osmo: It was a good time, and I definitely learned things there. The best was when he and I had a face-to-face conversation. But when Panula is in front of a crowd, he is somewhere else.

When you left the academy in 1979, were you ready to conquer the musical world?

Osmo: I had done my degree, I had done my paper work, and I felt like I was ready. I was able to do guest conducting, and I was able to read my scores. I thought guest conducting would happen first for me outside Helsinki. That would be one step, and then later on it would be great to have the Radio Orchestra or the Helsinki Philharmonic. During my time as a player at the Helsinki Philharmonic, I conducted some rehearsals and did some school concerts. So my feeling was, "I'd like to show what I can do, and hopefully I will be reinvited." And so it went, step by step.

It was that year that I first conducted the Helsinki Philharmonic in a regular concert. It was the Brahms Second Symphony. The principal oboe was a good friend of mine; he played the Strauss Oboe Concerto.

Then I went to some competitions and master classes. I was in Berlin in 1981, the Herbert von Karajan International Competition for Young Conductors, and I was out after the first round. Then I was in Sweden, at the Swedish Competition for Young Conductors; out after the second round. Then in 1982, I won the International Conducting Competition in Besançon, France. Actually, they gave two first prizes. The other went to a Japanese conductor. There are some very good names who have won that competition, so I thought that now this would open some doors for me, and it did—very slowly. But right after that I got my first foreign guest conducting opportunity in Poland and another in Norway, where I was with the Stavanger Orchestra for quite a few weeks over two years time. They called me their principal guest conductor without asking me.

Yes, it went slowly, slowly compared to Jukka-Pekka and Esa-Pekka, who made bigger steps. Then in 1985, I started in Lahti. And at the same time I had concerts in Sweden, Denmark, and Belgium. It was slow.

Was it a difficult decision to leave your secure job at the Helsinki Philharmonic Orchestra?

Osmo: I felt I had to make a decision, either to stay in the orchestra or leave, because I had gotten enough guest conducting invitations so that it was becoming difficult to do my job in the orchestra. It's not nice to keep asking for free weeks to go and conduct. There were some other young conductors in the orchestra at that time who needed to get some free time, and I felt that I shouldn't keep asking. So I had to decide. It's been said many times that you have to jump in and try to survive, whereas if you do only the safe things, you don't give enough. You believe at the moment that you can do it. Your faith is strong. I remember at that time, though, looking at my calendar, how few things I had going. But then it started. It was like a snowball. It was small, but it was moving. Then it got slightly bigger.

Was it difficult going from playing clarinet to conducting the Helsinki Philharmonic Orchestra? The players now have to see you not as a colleague but as a leader.

Osmo: When you go for the first time in front of a big orchestra, it's tough. The players can do whatever they want. It's easier with a smaller orchestra. But I was so young. I was thinking about this as such a good chance, so I didn't think so much about those risks. You believe that you can do it, and that helps you to do it. If you start to think only about the risks, that's when you make mistakes. And I also think when it's your own orchestra, their first reaction is to be helpful. Then if something goes wrong, they might be the biggest critics.

While serving as co-principal clarinet of the Helsinki Philharmonic Orchestra, Osmo began his conducting career.

"His performance of Carl Nielsen's eruptive Fifth Symphony . . . did much to confirm what earlier experience suggested, that Mr. Vänskä is indeed a master of Scandinavian music. . . . This is unquestionably a conductor to watch."

James Oestreich, *The New York Times*

Dreams Come True in Lahti

Osmo had extraordinary success with the Lahti Symphony Orchestra. This little orchestra—it was only forty players in 1985—and its promising but largely unknown conductor became internationally famous through recordings and tours. Though Osmo's career hadn't exactly lit up the sky in the six years since he left the Sibelius Academy, it seemed, at least in retrospect, that in taking the position in Lahti he was the right man at the right time. There would be a new team at the podium: Ulf Soderblom was coming in as chief conductor (replacing Jouko Saari), with Osmo serving as principal guest conductor. And Osmo, whose family now included three children, would continue living in Riihimäki, some forty-five miles north of Helsinki, where they had lived since Osmo took his position with the Helsinki Philharmonic Orchestra.

Osmo spoke of his twenty-three years at the helm of the Lahti orchestra.

Osmo and Leonidas Kavakos, with whom the Lahti Symphony Orchestra recorded Sibelius' Violin Concerto.

By all accounts, when you came to Lahti in 1985, the orchestra, wasn't in good shape.

Osmo: Yes, the players weren't happy. They wanted to get better.

You were well-schooled and eager but without a lot of experience.

Osmo: No one is experienced at the start. I had played clarinet for many years, but this was a new excitement, to start as a conductor, to try to do those things that a conductor does. Of course, there wasn't any guarantee at the time: How well can I do it? Do I have gasoline for the trip, or do I plummet? But I was really eager. When you are young you believe you know everything and are ready to do it all.

In 1988 you became music director, trading positions with Soderblom, who bowed out after another three years. Was that the plan from the start?

Osmo: That may have been part of his idea, to get the orchestra moving and then to step down. But I don't know if it was Soderblom who decided on me or if it was the orchestra. I know the idea was to get someone who was a serious conductor, as Soderblom was, and then have someone young, who might be talented, and to start them together. And there was a plan behind this, that Soderblom would accept the job if more players were added to the orchestra. And that happened. And then when I started there were to be even more added.

What was the level of playing during those first three years?

Osmo: Some concerts were good, some not so good. But we really tried. There was a lot of drive and a feeling of progress.

Say something about the Garage Discussions, the plan by which you and General Manager Tuomas Kinberg set out to build an orchestra team spirit.

Osmo: The traditional way in orchestras—and it's still true in many countries—is that the administration and the music director give ideas for the orchestra, and the orchestra criticizes those ideas. We wanted to avoid this kind of criticism in favor of a more positive attitude. For me, I've always thought that if someone has a criticism, that person believes that he or she knows how to do it better. If there are better ideas, is there a way to get them out? Another way to say it: I have one brain. It has capacity X. But if we can put ten people together, then the capacity of the brain is much larger. Or, we can put fifty people together, so that everyone is trying to come up with new ideas. If there's a problem, in other words, maybe we have a solution rather than just criticizing. That was the idea: to give people more freedom to say what they believe would be good for the orchestra, and then to actually try to do those things. It was a way of trying to commit people so that they have their own vision of the future.

When it started, some people were skeptical; they thought it would never work. But we made some good steps, and then more and more of the players began to understand that there

might be something good about this. Then it started to be part of a routine.

The teamwork concept didn't stop you from making the artistic decisions. Can the production of art really be a democratic process?

Osmo: The most obvious example is the rehearsal. The conductor has to tell the orchestra what to do and how to do it. There is no way to change that, or you can't accomplish anything. But even in rehearsal I try to create an atmosphere in which the players' ideas are welcome or they can ask me why we play it that way. And that helps me to be more logical in my decisions. But I think the programming also can be democratic. We had five to seven members in the programming committee, most of them musicians. At the same time it had to be understood that there must be someone who is making the final decisions, because art needs that. It's a complicated situation. If the boss is acting like a dictator and not listening to anyone, I don't think that's a good way. We tried to create an atmosphere—and I think we really did it—where people

The Lahti Symphony Orchestra with principal guest conductor Osmo Vänskä and chief conductor Ulf Soderblom.

were encouraged to bring ideas, and yet with the understanding that someone has to say, for instance, if they suggest three pieces on a program, there can't be three big symphonies. We have to come to a consensus.

The Lahti Symphony Orchestra sometimes played music at soccer games.

You wanted the Lahti orchestra to relate to the entire community. The orchestra played for soccer games and gave away a free recording of "Finlandia" to 10,000 people who lined up early one morning in front of a department store to get them, and you played a series in an old factory. What was behind this idea?

Osmo: The city was paying us. We were like the city's music department. We were serving the citizens of the city. The orchestra is not elitist. It's for everyone. We wanted to make that more commonly known—that it wasn't a big deal if you come and listen to us. Also, those 10,000 records were paid for by the Lahti companies that were supporting the orchestra. What we wanted to say was, "Hey, here we are. We are doing good things. We're trying to do something in a new way. Come and listen to us. And be aware that you have an orchestra in town that is going to serve you."

Did you bring more people in?

Osmo: Yes. We were trying to make a new image for the orchestra. We got more people to the concerts and many more simply aware of us. It's like the story of Solti and the Chicago Symphony. They were a huge success on that first European tour. There were people who never came to concerts, but they were so proud of their orchestra. Something similar happened in Lahti.

Why was the vote on building Sibelius Hall so close: 30 to 29?

Osmo: The number is not the whole story. I was guest conducting in Australia at the time of the vote. We arranged a time when they would call me with the result. When they called there was singing in the background, so I knew it had passed. See, we knew in advance who was in favor of the project and who wasn't, and the vote was in alphabetical order. Some were able to vote against it, so as to impress certain of their voters, even though they were in favor of it, and they knew it would pass. In other words, the hall never had a great majority, but it never was so bad as the vote numbers suggest.

The only thing I will add is that all the people who were against the project changed their minds when they finally saw the hall and especially now when they understand how much impact it has had on the city of Lahti. We were trying to make a new image for the orchestra.

It is said that there was envy in Helsinki of Lahti's success.

Osmo: Well, I think that envy has calmed down a little bit, but it really was there. It's a small country. Many were so used to putting Helsinki at the top and everyone else way down. In fact, some of those way down were trying new things. Others believe that things are always going to be as they were a hundred years ago or fifty years ago, but we didn't believe that. We tried to play just as well as the best.

Actually, we weren't playing against Helsinki or anyone else. When we play in Minnesota, too, we try to play as well as possible. But it's not against Chicago. It's not against New York. It's not against anyone. It's just our way to do music. And the same thing happened in Lahti. We weren't happy with how things were before. We wanted to do better. There are always big boys, and the big boys don't like it when some smaller boys are doing better.

Does the Lahti orchestra have a unique, identifiable sound?

Osmo: Yes. It comes in the tutti sound. It has never had a large string section. This means you have always to be careful so that the brass players—and sometimes even the woodwinds—don't sound too loud. It's a transparent sound. I think of it like a scrim that you find in a theater. You can see through it. There are lights behind it. If it's thick, you don't hear things that could be very exciting. Well, of course, when we come to a fortissimo, it should be as thick as possible.

Why isn't it more brass-heavy?

Osmo: That's my style, and it has been that way here, too, with the Minnesota Orchestra. I always want to have this kind of rounded brass sound, a sound that isn't violent. I never want them to scream. I want to keep the beauty of the sound, some kind of noble sound. When you don't go to the loudest, that helps the intonation. And the players can hear each other better when they don't play so loud.

As you look back on your twenty-three years in Lahti, what stands out in your memory?

Osmo: I'm very grateful for all those years, that I was able to learn my job in so many of its aspects: on-stage and off-stage and all the politics of it. The Lahti time has been the biggest school for me. I think that I went through all the possible problems that you could run into as a conductor. Lahti was so important a time in my life. But it was also good that I was able to leave when I did. It was time to look to the future. And I'm so happy that I have the Minnesota Orchestra. I have a lot of opportunities with this great orchestra. It was a long time in Lahti, longer than for many conductors. Leaving was a sad thing.

You won't be going back for a while?

Osmo: They need to understand that I am away, and the audience needs to understand that, too. But I am an honorary conductor, so I will go back there. But, for now, I need some time to breathe.

Iceland and Scotland

Within a decade after taking over the Lahti Symphony Orchestra, Osmo's career began to expand outside Finland. In 1993, in addition to his Lahti post, he became chief conductor of the Iceland Symphony Orchestra, a relatively young orchestra—founded in 1950—that gave a regular subscription series in Reykjavik and toured both inside Iceland and to key cities in Europe. His three-year term ended on an up beat with a U.S. tour that concluded with a Carnegie Hall concert in February 1996. Though the hall was just half full, the review in *The New York Times* by Alex Ross described this as Vänskä's "sensational Carnegie Hall debut" and went on to call him "a real master of orchestral drama who produced one of the finest Sibelius performances I have encountered." (This had also been Osmo's United States debut as a conductor.)

Looking back on those three years, Osmo lauded the orchestra in Reykjavik. "Those people really wanted to work, and I still have some good friends there. It was a great adventure for me, first of all to see a very different country. It was like going to the moon, but the people were very friendly. And it was my first position with a foreign orchestra. It isn't a big country, but the position wasn't unimportant. I learned many things about my job there. And the America tour was important. It opened doors. I enjoyed my time in Reykjavik, but also it was clear that I wasn't going to be there a long time."

That same winter Osmo signed on as chief conductor of the BBC Scottish Symphony Orchestra, one of four BBC (British Broadcasting Corporation) symphony orchestras in Great Britain, an engagement that over the course of six years would not only revitalize the orchestra but would make Osmo one of the most admired conductors working regularly in Great Britain, a hit with audiences and a favorite with the English press.

As had been the case with the Lahti orchestra when Osmo arrived, the BBC Scottish Symphony Orchestra, by the early 1990s, had hit the skids. According to Hugh Macdonald, who was director of that orchestra then, "Orchestra morale had dropped, vacant positions had not been filled, and the previous principal conductor, Jerzy Maksymiuk, whose

Osmo and Pirkko Vänskä with the fifth president of the Republic of Iceland, Ólafur Ragnar Grimsson.

contract had ended in 1992, had not been replaced." A typical review from that time—Christopher Lambton writing in the *Sunday Times* of London—paints a dire picture: "Under the incomprehensible Jerzy Maksymiuk, orchestral standards declined so much that the entire cello section, it was rumored, had been sent on a training course. I heard one broadcast performance of a Brahms symphony that sounded like a school orchestra in rehearsal." Given the circumstances, Macdonald's job was to try to rebuild the orchestra's confidence and, most important, to find a new chief conductor.

"We had heard on the grapevine about a Finnish conductor who was not yet known much outside Scandinavia but was beginning to make his mark, not least through some excellent Sibelius recordings with his orchestra in Lahti," Macdonald recalled. In 1994 he invited Osmo, on short notice, to conduct the BBC Scottish Orchestra in a studio concert played to a small audience in the orchestra's studio in Glasgow. The program included Nielsen's Symphony No. 2. "It was very clear from the energy and edge-of-the-seat excitement that Osmo brought to the Nielsen that here was a conductor who instinctively knew how to inspire and motivate our players," Macdonald said. "My colleagues and I were convinced that this indeed could be the man we were looking for."

But he wanted to see how Osmo and the orchestra would work together on a big stage, and so he offered him a date on one of the world's biggest—the BBC Proms at Royal Albert Hall in London. The orchestra was booked for three Proms appearances in the summer of 1995. Osmo agreed to the engagement, after which he and Macdonald worked out a program that would be heavy on Sibelius, opening with "Finlandia" and concluding with the Fifth Symphony.

In addition to Osmo's public identification with Jean Sibelius, the Finnish composer's music had long been in the forefront of the orchestra's repertoire, going back nearly to its beginnings in 1935 and its founder, Ian Whyte, who had a special love of Sibelius. In fact, part of the orchestra's lore is that Sibelius heard one of Whyte's broadcasts of his Symphony No. 1 on the BBC during World War II and was so impressed that he sent Whyte a telegram of congratulation.

Osmo's Proms concert was a success. For audience and orchestra, this was a new, less romanticized reading of Sibelius: darker, more detailed, even harsh at times. The music critic of the *Times*, Hilary Finch, described the performance as "revelatory." As Macdonald recalled, "At the end Osmo left the stage in tears, the bravos ringing in his ears. The concert had all the London critics sitting up to take notice of both conductor and orchestra, not a situation we, the BBC orchestra located furthest from the powerful (and sometimes snooty) international metropolitan music scene of London, were used to. And Osmo from that moment on was established as a firm favorite of the Proms audience."

Macdonald met with Osmo's Finnish agent, Tuula Sarotie, and worked out an initial three-year contract that would start at the beginning of the 1996-1997 season with a commitment of twelve to fourteen weeks a year. And shortly thereafter, he spent a day with Osmo and Pirkko at their home in Riihimäki, getting acquainted and making plans. Since they knew that Sibelius' music would draw an audience, they put together a series, "The Sibelius Experience," and mixed that with ample lesser-known repertoire, both new and old, all to be given at the acoustically bright Glasgow City Hall. For the opening concert, attended by the Finnish ambassador and his wife, Pekka Kuusisto played the Sibelius Violin Concerto, and Osmo conducted the same composer's Symphony No. 1. At the end, as Macdonald remembers it, "The audience went wild." All the subsequent concerts that season were sold out, something this orchestra hadn't experienced in several years. "Suddenly everyone was talking about Osmo and the BBC Scottish Symphony Orchestra,"

said Macdonald. "The players were walking on air, not quite believing what was happening. They were used to the orchestra playing second fiddle to the Royal Scottish National Orchestra, the other orchestra in Glasgow that had leapt to international fame under the exciting, though brief, tenure of Neeme Järvi."

BBC Scottish Symphony programs in subsequent seasons included Rachmaninoff and Nielsen cycles. The six Nielsen symphonies were eventually recorded for BIS. For the Hyperion label, they recorded Anton Bruckner's Third Symphony. A Beethoven cycle titled "Beethoven the Revolutionary" included a concert made up of the composer's first three symphonies, an evening with two intermissions. And as far as new and recent works, the orchestra made a specialty of Scottish composer James MacMillan's music; its recording of MacMillan's "The Confession of Isobel Gowdie" received a Gramophone Award. In addition, they toured to small towns in Scotland and big cities throughout Europe, and their impressive performance of Beethoven's Symphony No. 7 at Symphony Hall in Boston during the orchestra's first United States tour gave Osmo's reputation in America a significant boost. The orchestra's success in those years with Osmo, who eventually renewed his contract for another three years, created a momentum on the home front to initiate the long-hoped-for rebuilding of City Hall, an expensive project that needed city council approval. The result, now one of Britain's most admired concert halls, was unveiled in 2006.

Osmo during his tenure with the BBC Scottish Symphony Orchestra

By early 2001, people were contemplating the end of the Vänskä era in Glasgow. Michael Tumelty, critic of the city's daily newspaper, the *Herald*, quoted Macdonald as saying that Osmo would be "less available" after that season and that he had "one or two people in mind" as Osmo's successor. He

were full of high praise, even though some of the musicians in the orchestra made it clear that Osmo had worked them harder than they preferred and they were glad to see him leave. Tumelty, on the other hand, likened Osmo's influence on the orchestra to an electrical charge that galvanizes everything it touches—what he called "the Vänskä effect." "The technical honing and transformation of the BBC Scottish Symphony Orchestra under Vänskä's stewardship was never beyond description, but, at its best, still beggared belief," Tumelty wrote. "The musical revelations across a range of repertoire, even to sophisticated ears, have been breathtaking."

The BBC Scottish Symphony with conductor Osmo Vänskä.

reported that European orchestras were showing an interest in Osmo, and Jasper Parrott of the Harrison Parrott management firm predicted publicly that Osmo would hold a major principal conductor post within five years. Tumelty quoted veteran players in the Cleveland Orchestra who claimed that Osmo was "the most interesting conductor" they had seen since George Szell.

A year later, in March 2002, when Osmo officially relinquished his title with the orchestra in a final series of concerts, the inevitable ruminations in the press on the Vänskä years

Looking back on those years, Osmo said he knew that some of the musicians felt overworked, even though they didn't make their complaints to him. "What strikes me more," he said, "is that the timing was perfect. It was six years altogether in Glasgow. I had told them in the fourth year that I wasn't going to renew my contract. There was one summer there that I thought, though this had been an important place for me, it was time to stop. I had come to realize that this is no one's orchestra. The problem in Scotland is that they have many, many guest conductors because they also have to do all these studio broadcasts, which means it's not just the orchestra that does planning. It's also Radio 3 in London, which says you have to record all these works during the season. The BBC owns the orchestra. So I felt that I couldn't create those things that I had done, for example, in Lahti, where I was much more involved. As a result, I felt, even though there had been so many positive things there, it was time for me to go on to something else, even though at that time I had no invitations from any other orchestras."

By all accounts, Osmo did a lot to raise both the visibility and the prestige of the BBC Scottish Symphony Orchestra during his six years there, but his own career benefited, too, by giving him a presence in Great Britain. An added plus—and another example of good timing—came early in his Glasgow period: He signed with the international management office of Harrison Parrott. Osmo's manager Lydia Connolly recalled, "There was word coming out of Finland, where we've always had good contacts and colleagues, that Osmo might be interested in talking to us. An introduction was arranged through a third party in Finland, and Jasper Parrott visited Osmo in Lahti. The timing was right," Connolly said. "Osmo was ready to go in a new direction, and I was recently back from my second maternity leave and was re-building my list of artists." They signed a contract in 1998.

In earlier years, Osmo had been represented by a small London agency. But he was eager to step up a notch or two. He made inquiries at some of the bigger management offices, asking, "What can I do to get better orchestras as a guest conductor?" He was treated politely, but no one would take him on. Though he thinks of himself as an optimist, Osmo admits that in the early 1990s he couldn't help noticing that his schoolmates, Salonen and Saraste, had made impressive career leaps—Salonen to the Los Angeles Philharmonic, Saraste to the Toronto Symphony—while he was still in Lahti. And even though the Lahti recordings were winning awards, his own career looked to be stalled, which left him wondering if he was doing something wrong. "I wouldn't call this a dark period," he said. "But it was some kind of shadow. I wasn't bitter toward those guys," he said, referring to Salonen and Saraste. "They really did good work. I just wondered why it wasn't happening for me. I simply wanted things to go faster. Only later did I understand that a slower pace was very good for me. But I didn't see that back then. For example, people kept saying that the Lahti orchestra was playing better because of me, but maybe I didn't see how much better they were playing. Another way to put it: I knew they were playing better, but I wasn't so sure if that image was being conveyed outside Finland. Right now, it's fine. It's great to realize how many really big things actually happened in Lahti. But when it's happening, you don't see it.

In 1991, Osmo and the Lahti Symphony Orchestra won the Gramophone Record of the Year Award with their recording of Sibelius' Violin Concerto. Robert von Bahr, president of BIS, is at the microphone.

"I thought that I had the gifts to be a good conductor, and I started to think, 'Is this some kind of unrealistic dream for me? Maybe I'm never going to get there.' And this thought went on for a long time. I think that we all want to do work on a little bit higher level. When you feel that people aren't recognizing you, then you start to conduct as if you are trying to prove that you can do good things, and that's unhealthy. You try too hard, and then you're not relaxed. Those are the symptoms of that kind of thinking: 'Why don't I get better agencies?' This is easy to speak about now, but even so, I can't help thinking, what if I had never gotten the BBC Scottish Symphony? If from Lahti I had to go to an even smaller city. But, in fact, my dream came true. I'm happy. I'm lucky. I'm thankful."

From a manager's point of view, what did Osmo's career need in 1998? What was missing? "It was the international presence and recognition," Connolly said. "He was right on the cusp. He was already due to go to Cleveland. And, of course, the Lahti recordings were a significant calling card. And I should add that we weren't trying to reduce the Lahti commitment. We weren't trying to get him out of there in order to expand his guest conducting. Lahti was—and continued to be—a significant part of who he was." Among the early bookings she arranged were the Chicago Symphony Orchestra, the Orchestre de Paris, the Berlin Philharmonic, and the Royal Concertgebouw. "He's been asked back everywhere except the Concertgebouw," she said. And why not the Concertgebouw? "There have been times when he's gone to an orchestra where the players haven't enjoyed the hard work, and that hasn't resulted in another invitation because neither side thought it was necessary to repeat the experience, and that's fine. Chemistry is such an elusive but crucial part of this."

One of those early bookings, in October 2000, was a week's worth of concerts with the Minnesota Orchestra. Little did anyone know as that week started that just seven months later, Osmo and the orchestra would hold a significant press conference. Jasper Parrott's prediction that Osmo would hold a major principal conductor post was very shrewd indeed.

"The Sibelius, unsurprisingly, brought out the best in Vänskä,
as he, in turn, encouraged the players of the BBC Symphony
to play with an energy, a force, and a commitment that presented them at their best."

Matthew Rye, London *Daily Telegraph*

The Vänskä Family

The Vänskäs' first child, daughter Tytti, was born in 1976; a year after that Osmo accepted the job of co-principal clarinet at the Helsinki Philharmonic. Partly because they were short of money at the time, the Vänskäs settled not in Helsinki but in a house in Riihimäki, a forty-five-minute train ride from the capital city, It was there that they raised their children, including their two sons, Olli and Perttu.

In 1985, around the time Osmo took the job of principal guest conductor with the Lahti Symphony, Pirkko gave up nursing, partly to take care of their youngest son, Perttu, who was born with a heart condition that had required a complicated operation.

The Vanskas have raised a family of performers. Tytti is an actress specializing in music theater in Kouvola, Finland. She has enjoyed success on the stage in recent years, and they have a collection of rave reviews to prove it. The sons are musicians. Both Olli and Perttu have been playing the violin since they were four and five years old. Perttu started playing the double bass when he was a little older.

Olli is in graduate school studying musicology. He plays electric violin in a heavy-metal band, Turisas. Perttu, who has a degree from the Helsinki Pop and Jazz Conservatory, is also a musicology student and a composer, arranger, and producer.

"My attitude was always that I would advise them [in their career choices] but that they would have to make their own decisions," says Osmo. "I told them I would support whatever they are doing. Music has always been a part of their lives, but I never pushed them toward being musicians, and I certainly never started out with the idea, like 'you have to be a lawyer or whatever.' They have to lead their own lives. But I am really happy with what they are doing. They are wonderful kids.

"Since Olli plays electric violin in a band, Turisas, I have learned a few things about this music that I didn't know before. I had a rough idea about this metal kind of music. Twice I have been to their gigs, and I have listened to their CD and have seen their DVD. They have fun. They've had a number of tours, some in the U.S. They're recording another CD. They are very serious about their music, and Olli is giving a lot to the band. He enjoys it. What could be better for the father? I'm sure he won't be doing this forever. But this will give

The Vänskä home in Riihimäki, Finland.

him so many good skills and will teach him about this business. Without this experience with Turisas, he wouldn't be the same guy. With a BBA degree in International Business from the Lahti University of Applied Sciences, he has a good education in finance as well as music. This experience is giving him a practical example in how to go on the road with a band.

The Vänskä family celebrating a Minnesota Orchestra performance at Finlandia Hall in Helsinki: (left to right) Malla Vivolin (Perttu's girlfriend), Perttu, Tytti, Olli, Osmo, Pirkko.

"Perttu played double bass, but now electric guitar is his instrument. He is working more and more as a producer and arranger with his studio recording work. Perttu is also a gifted composer."

A Daughter's Thoughts

In observance of Osmo's official goodbye to the Lahti Symphony in May 2008, at which time he stepped down as chief conductor, the daily newspaper in Lahti, *Etela-Suomen Sanomat*, asked several people close to the conductor to an-

swer five questions about him. One of those questioned was Osmo's daughter, Tytti. Here are the questions and her answers.

When and where did you get to know Osmo?

"Osmo was not there to hear my first scream, but he's been very good about hearing me cry and scream many times over the years. I'm totally 'Daddy's girl,' so I know him very well, in good and bad."

Why have Vänskä and the Lahti orchestra been such good partners?

"I haven't been there all that time, but I would say that behind everything is love. The orchestra and Osmo have grown together and have a good relationship. In that relationship, you can watch each other in both good days and bad."

What quality makes Vänskä a top conductor?

"He was given talent, but I think besides that he's the person who works the most. I don't know anybody else who works harder, and nothing goes ahead of the work. He tells funny stories, looks you in the eyes, and can be nice. Sometimes I'm so envious."

Has this international fame, being on top of the world, changed Vänskä as a human being?

"No."

Does his public identity correspond with his real character?

"I don't know about his public image. Osmo is super-good in his work, and I'm really proud of him."

A Finn in Minnesota

"When we got to Lahti, I looked around, and the deal finally made sense," David Hyslop, former Minnesota Orchestra president, said on traveling to Finland to sign Osmo to a Minnesota contract. "Lahti looks like Minnesota."

How is life different for you in Minneapolis compared to Finland? Do people relate to you differently here?

Osmo: In Finland and the Nordic countries everyone wants to be so democratic. So they're very negative about anyone who is different or doing different things or is doing better than others. Everyone is supposed to be equal. Whereas, here it's totally different. There's much more space, more freedom. The attitude is: Do what you can and enjoy it. In Finland, there's a lot of envy. If a Finn buys a new car, the neighbors are really envious. "Who does he think he is? He tries to be better than others, and that's *terrible*!" Whereas, here, if your neighbor gets a new car, you say, "If that is possible for him, maybe it's possible for me, too." You never say that in Finland and, if you do, people will really hate you. It doesn't matter what you have done to earn it. They might smile very tightly for you, but they will be thinking, "Why is he trying to show everybody how good he is?" It's a huge difference. We say that envy is one of the natural resources in Finland. It grows very strongly. And, by the way, this is not only my opinion. Many people have observed this. It's a killer because it's so negative. It means that people are watching each other.

It's like they're saying, "I can't do anything, and I'm so happy that my neighbor can't do anything either." They're saying, "Let's stay down," instead of, "Let's try to do something."

Connected to this is the way people support their children. Here they are always willing to give good feedback, and that is really different from Finland. And that has been one of my problems here. I think the musicians got frustrated because I would just tell what was wrong. What I didn't understand is that I have to say, "Thank you" and "Great job." They don't do that in Finland. There, if it's OK, you don't say anything. On the other hand, if it wasn't good, you get angry and say what's wrong. Of course, I am exaggerating. But this is a huge difference. For instance, we were at the church here, and we heard a children's choir. Obviously, they were a group who had practiced maybe only once or twice. I know what would have been the reaction in Finland. They would have been told to practice more. Here the reaction was, "Oh, wonderful. It was so great. Thanks for doing that." I know these kids

Finland or Minnesota?

had no idea whether it was good or bad. But they will remember what people said afterwards, that compliment. They will be proud of that, and the next time they sing, they will have more confidence. In Finland they would have heard that they were nothing and maybe that they shouldn't even come here again. And that is what they will remember, that they weren't good. So their confidence goes down, and the next time they're scared to perform. This is one of the biggest things I have learned here, and it's not connected just to children but to the whole system. You remember here to say, "Great job. Well done." That's all it takes.

You are often complimentary to the players when something has gone well.

Osmo: I try to do that, though I remember when we were rehearsing for the second tour, some people from the orchestra got really upset with me. They said, "It's like we can't do anything right. All you say is, 'We can't do this; we can't do that.'" So I know I'm not good at that, but I try to give positive feedback. I have learned so much about those things here, and I have to say that it's so much better when the general attitude is positive.

You are a local celebrity. Do people seated nearby whisper your name in a restaurant?

Osmo: I recognize that people know me, and sometimes I'm a little bit embarrassed. But I also have to say that people can do it the right way so that it's natural, and, of course, I have to accept my role in this community. On the other hand, if no one knows me, then something is wrong with the relationship of the orchestra with the community.

You are a member at Central Lutheran Church in downtown Minneapolis. I hear that even when you have a concert on Saturday night, you attend an early service the next morning at the church.

Osmo: Yes, I like the church, and I would like to go there even more often. Sometimes it's not possible when I'm traveling. But I would have to say it's a good place to go.

Your English is good. Do you think in Finnish?

Osmo: Very much. Languages aren't my best part. But I know more and more English, and right now I'm working on that. I read the newspaper aloud every morning. I haven't done it enough, but I'm working at it.

I have both Finnish and English books, but mostly I read in Finnish because it goes so much faster. It takes a lot of energy and time for me to read in English. But I try to find texts in English that are not so complicated. We have a lot of Finnish books at home. There have been one or two examples where I have read something in Finnish, then I read the same thing in English, and that's good because then I'm not totally lost if I don't understand something. The problem so often isn't that I don't know the words, but that you say the same thing in such a different way in English than you would in Finnish. If I translate into English the Finnish way of saying something, like a joke, no one understands it. Then I learn to say the same thing in English, but it comes out like a different idea, even though the purpose is exactly the same.

J started running for health reasons in 1999 and to keep in better shape. I really enjoy running, as it gives me time alone to work off stress and time alone to think. When traveling, I always have my running stuff with me. Bicycling is the newest thing for me. I recently bought a new hi-tech bicycle, and it's another great way to keep in shape.

On the plane are you reading your scores or a book?

Osmo: Usually, when I am traveling to work in another city, I might be looking at scores to check things I have to conduct the next day, whereas when I am coming back, I wouldn't have scores in front of me. But a book is always with me, and sometimes two, in case I finish the first one. A computer is with me, too, but I don't use it very often. I might talk to someone sitting next to me and then hand out a CD, but I'm not a very extroverted person.

You turned down a series of concerts with the New York Philharmonic because you had a church concert commitment here.

Osmo: It was the new bell tower at Central Lutheran Church that was going to be dedicated, and they hired the Minnesota Orchestra to play at the opening ceremony. I promised to conduct, and Stephen Paulus wrote a piece for it. It was a unique situation. Plus, I'm a member of the congregation here, so I just felt this was an important thing for me to do. If I promise something, I have to do it.

Osmo encounters fellow Finns during short tours with the orchestra to small towns in Minnesota. (The state boasts nearly 100,000 Finns among its predominately German and Scandinavian population.) For example, tickets for the orchestra's February 2005 performance in Cokato, a western Minnesota town of 2,727 people, sold out almost immediately. As might be expected, there were a lot of Finns in attendance that night at the town's new performing arts center. Columnist Chuck Haga quoted Vänskä in the *Star Tribune* during the trip, which included concerts in Northfield, Windom, Sauk Centre, and Willmar. "They come and say hello and tell about themselves," said Vänskä. "Some speak Finnish very well, and that's nice to hear. Even if they don't know so many words, it shows they value their connection to Finland.

"I have heard many times that my job means very much to them. They are sometimes in tears when they say it, and then I am in tears. It is very touching."

What is it that makes a world-famous conductor leave the podium, exit the stage door, jump onto a motorcycle, turn the key—HARUMFF, HARUMFF—and zoom off into the night, leaving swirling eddies of dust and debris in his wake? Conductors are supposed to slip quietly into a waiting limousine, frenzied applause still ringing in their ears.

Osmo does have a car, though it's not a limousine. When the weather's decent, he prefers his motorcycle, and it's a big one—a Yamaha V-Star 650. It gets him around the city, but also out of the city. In September 2008, for instance, he drove to Thunder Bay, Canada. "It was six-and-a-half hours coming back," he said, "Three-and-a-half hours in rain. That was tough because the road got slipperier and slipperier."

"It's the feeling of freedom." Osmo said. "You are alone and away from telephones. For a little while at least. Also the motorcycle is powerful. There is this element of danger, and you have to handle it so that you don't take too many risks. That's one thing I've learned: Don't assume that car drivers can see you. You have to be ready to escape whatever happens."

Just for the record, the conductor always wears a helmet.

HARUMFF, HARUMFF.

"*Without the church
and music and museums,
the world would be a terrible place.*"

Osmo Vänskä

Minnesota
Orchestra

Hard at Work

Vänskä has a formidable work ethic.
"Verk, verk, verk" has become a catch phrase
among musicians at the Minnesota Orchestra.

Wielding the Baton

Osmo Vänskä brings a unique power and delicacy to the music he conducts. He cites his devotion to the composer, and he is fastidious, even obsessive, in his fidelity to the scores in front of him.

You use a baton most of the time, but sometimes you put it down.

Osmo: Someone might have different opinions about this, but when there is no need for a big pulse and no need to keep up a tempo, I think I can do more with my hands. It gives me more freedom and, I hope, more freedom for the players, too. But for the players in the back, I think they can see better when I have a baton.

It is said that an orchestra facing a new conductor knows within minutes whether he or she is any good. Do you make a speech when you face an orchestra of strangers?

Osmo: Never a speech. Orchestras hate conductors who give speeches. I remember that from my years playing in an orchestra. It should be all on the music. We start to play and then begin to put things together, and I show them how I would like it to go. The more you can do with body language and arms rather than with speech, the better it is.

What the conductor is doing is a reflection of his personality or charisma. Can you believe him or is there something about him that you cannot trust? That's the thing that happens between an orchestra and a conductor. It isn't a question of whether a conductor makes some small mistakes, but whether he is making real music.

When an orchestra is playing, it's a question of how much the players will give you. If the conductor doesn't win them to his side, they might just play correctly—but nothing more. A good conductor will invite them to make music, and then they will give more. So, in other words, to invite is not to be a dictator but to say, "We make music together." That's what I try to do. If someone acts as a dictator, it might work. But it's better if they really want to do it rather than the conductor commanding that they do it.

A conductor should have all the musical skills: an ear for intonation, a feeling for pulse. You need to have those things. You might learn to use them better, but if you don't already have them, you cannot go and buy them. We learn through experience, by making mistakes. But I need to have those skills inside me. What teaching does is bring them out. The talent must already be there.

The rhythmical things have always been easy for me. If you don't have an understanding of rhythm, then you're in trouble. So when someone goes to school, they can't rebuild your rhythmical understanding or your understanding of tempos. If you have to do sixty, but you're always doing ninety-two, it doesn't work.

> "A conductor should have all the musical skills: an ear for intonation, a feeling for pulse. You might learn to use them better, but if you don't already have them, you cannot go and buy them."
>
> Osmo Vänskä

Maybe I have needed more time to let the music breathe, so that I am not forcing it, like I have a whip. In time, you realize that you don't need to use a whip. I also think I have been good at recognizing what goes wrong in a performance or what's starting to go wrong. I have always noticed where I have to go to fix something.

What the orchestra recognizes right away, I think, is whether the conductor can keep a good pulse and how his hands are working. Is he easy to follow? Can they play together working with him? It involves hundreds of details. Does the conductor encourage them to do things? Or does he hesitate, in which case the orchestra will hesitate. Another thing: Does the conductor make musical phrases rather than just beating time—1, 2, 3, 4. And does the conductor indicate accents and dynamics?

Then it's a question of how you work with other musicians. How do you communicate? If everyone is against you, forget the whole thing. It doesn't matter if you know everything in the world, if you are unable to work with anyone. But that kind of thing you can learn. You can change your behavior if you are smart enough or if you have smart friends who will tell you what you are doing wrong. But if you have problems with your pulse, with finding the right tempo and keeping it, then it's impossible. This understanding of pulse must be somewhere within you.

It is said that there are many great orchestras but fewer great conductors. Does that have something to do with training?

Osmo: I really don't know the best way to train conductors. It never works if you simply go to school and someone tries to make you a good conductor. You cannot learn conducting without conducting. You can't learn it from a book. There must be so much in a person already, and then the school could give you some points, but there is not enough time for the school to teach you everything. To be a good conductor there are some things that are important.

You need to play at least one instrument first. You don't need to be an international soloist, but you need to be at the professional level before you can understand the things that a conductor needs. That's one part of a conductor's training—learning your instrument.

Saraste was the co-principal second violin in the Finnish Radio Symphony. And Salonen was a horn player. He never auditioned for a job, but he played substitute in the Radio Orchestra, the Philharmonic, and the Opera Orchestra. That's one common thing for almost all Finnish conductors.

They have a strong instrumental background, and they have played in professional orchestras, either as members or substitutes. That background gives you some kind of advantage.

It's also a matter of language. If you have played in an orchestra, you understand the language of the orchestra: how this crowd is communicating, what kind of tensions might be there, what the wind player might think about the violinists, and so on. It's a long step from the chair to the podium, but it's much, much longer if you haven't been inside the orchestra.

I have always been interested in what the conductor was doing. I would see things sometimes that the conductor didn't even know was a mistake. It was just something that wasn't working. That's another difference between good and bad conductors. Some believe, "I am doing great things," but everyone else thinks he's terrible. Other times I would see something that was really good, and I would try to remember it. With the others, it wasn't so much mistakes as it was whether the person was able to really use the time. The time factor is always there. We don't have eternal rehearsals. You have to use your time very effectively. The good conductor is the person who can find out very quickly the solution to the problem. Or I heard something that was out of tune. Will the conductor give any attention to that? Maybe he didn't even hear it, or he's not going to deal with that problem right away. Those kind of things I was recognizing there.

There's an old saying that the orchestra trains the conductor. The orchestra sounds as good as its conductor. In other words, there are not good or bad orchestras, only good and bad conductors. An orchestra can get a much better sound from a good conductor, and a bad conductor will get a lesser sound from the orchestra. It goes both ways. The orchestra is an instrument, and the conductor is playing that instrument. So you play with whatever skills you have, and it sounds either good or bad.

For example, I played one or two times with an old Italian conductor, Carlo Cecchi. He was quite good. At the Helsinki Philharmonic, especially in Finlandia Hall, the woodwinds often were slightly behind the strings. We would start a little late, in other words. He had the best technique for fixing this. The usual way would be for the conductor to say, "You are behind. Play earlier." But Cecchi recognized the problem right away in the first rehearsal. What he did was start to smile and then rotate his arms toward us. He was telling us with his body language, "Come in. Join us." Ever since, that has been one of the best lessons for me in how to handle this problem.

During the next season I was playing first clarinet, and conductor Cecchi didn't arrive. He was supposed to be at his hotel the prior night, but they couldn't find him, and we really needed this rehearsal. So the general manager came to me and said, "Could you do the rehearsal today? Then we can find

out where he is." If something happens, orchestras call agencies and try to find someone who is ready to do this program or sometimes they have to change the program. But, in this case, I was there. And I said, "Of course, yes." The next morning I got a phone call. He wasn't coming. He was ill. That was one of my first conducting experiences with the Philharmonic.

Some of the Lahti musicians say you were very clear at the podium right from the start and easy to follow, but that as time went on you became more economical in your gestures and, in a sense, simpler. Did you work on becoming more precise?

Osmo: It wasn't something I planned. But when you do something again and again, you start to feel that things are going well without having to jump always. Jumping makes you tired, so you don't want to do that if you don't have to. It is a question of not only how the conductor makes progress, but also how the orchestra progresses. If the instrumentalists play better, I don't need to be so involved. When we start rehearsing something, I have to do more than just "1-2-3-4."

As we move toward the concert, I might be doing less physically but more of other things. And that's true for all of us, I think. When we learn something, when we have had good and bad experiences, we come to understand more, and when we understand more, we don't need to make so much smoke. Also, if you get better and if you know the people have noticed that you have gotten better, then you don't have to prove something. That's one thing I remember: When I was a young conductor going to some place, I was so enthused and I wanted to do everything and prove to them that "hey, please recognize that I'm good and I can do things." This is something you can put aside when you are well known, which means you can concentrate on the music. You don't need to prove anything. You have all these experiences to draw from.

Tuomas Kinberg, manager of the Lahti Symphony Orchestra, said he talked to you once about your anger when the musicians made mistakes. Did it take a while to correct or did you change quickly?

Osmo: It was some kind of "Eureka!" Maybe a few things changed quickly. But some things are connected to your personality, and those are the most complicated things to change. That is, you know something in your brain, but then you are doing things without knowing what you are doing, because it comes from your personality and the way your temper is.

Because of this problem I had—I still have it sometimes—if I can't get good results quickly from the orchestra, I get angry and frustrated. Ideally, in rehearsal you can make corrections and fix things. But what if the players aren't able to change quickly and fix things? That's the point where I have to be careful. What happens is I start to think that they are playing against me, because they don't change what I ask for. Then I start to think that this must be because they are angry with me, and they are trying to insult me. Of course, if the chemistry isn't right, that could be the case. But I learned something important from Kinberg in Lahti. We just sat down one day after a rehearsal, and Tuomas said, "Osmo, you have to remember one thing. These are difficult things for the players, and we need some time to learn them. No one is playing wrongly on purpose." This was big news for me. I know that sounds stupid when I say it. But there was some kind of block. My thinking had become blocked. I had gotten more angry and aggressive feelings: "Why don't they play better?" What Tuomas said was important. I had to re-think this: "Hey, that's true. They try to do their best, and I'm not giving them enough time. Actually, what I am doing is poisoning the atmosphere." So it was really important, and I think that since then I have been a different conductor.

But it's still connected to my personality. If something goes wrong, I still can feel it very easily in my mind. If I can recognize any player who isn't giving 100 percent or is being lazy, this is the shortest way to get me really mad. What I learned—and what I want to learn more—is how to balance all these demands. I need to try to relax and to give the players more time. At those points when we have troubles, instead of saying, "Faster, faster" or "Slower, slower," it would be better to say, "Let's try to create this kind of sound picture" or whatever. I need work on those kinds of things—not giving an order but to simply invite them in.

Being a clarinetist watching the parade of conductors in Turku and Helsinki must have been like a school. What was the level of conductors you worked with in those years?

Osmo: We had some very good ones. Charles Dutoit was there, and Neville Marriner, [Raphael] Frühbeck de Burgos, and Mariss Jansons, and his father, Arvid, who also was a great teacher. He sometimes came to the Sibelius Academy. Mariss was a young guy when he started, and everyone liked his father very much. In a season, we would have four or five really high caliber conductors. The interesting thing is that from one conductor you can learn both good and bad things. Of course, it's a question of personal taste, too—not just what I happen to like but what I believe is good technique for the orchestra. One guy, for instance, could be doing some things in a good way, but he might be doing something else in a bad way. It's all variations. I believe that the worst of them have some good points that you can learn. All in all, it was a good time for me—good conductors and good colleagues.

Also, I got a grant to study two summers in Lucerne. In one summer I studied with Rafael Kubelik. He was great. He had a master class there that became so famous that they accepted only five or six students there. We all learned so much

from him. I was just starting out as a conductor. And in the same hall, we heard two programs—the Berlin Philharmonic with Herbert von Karajan and the Philadelphia Orchestra with Riccardo Muti. We got cheap tickets for these and saw all the top people.

Most of what I learned from Paavo Berglund I really respect. He never compromises, and that's what people say about me, I guess, that I don't do compromises. That's my strong point and my weak point also, because I want things exactly a certain way and nothing else. And I know that someone who demands so much could be tiring. It means doing it again and again and again. But I have learned this from Berglund, and it's so important. I think Muti is a good example of someone who is able to get exactly what he wants from an orchestra. And I saw a televised concert once by Carlo Giulini. He was someone who really respected his players. Think about Muti and Giulini, both Italian but so different.

Robert Kajanus was the father of us all. He founded the Helsinki Philharmonic, and he kept it going—sometimes with his own money. He was a friend of Sibelius, and he really started orchestra life in Finland. I regard him very highly. He made the first recordings of Sibelius. His recording of the First Symphony is really something. It's wild and dangerous, like a real bear, whereas for most conductors now it's very tame and mild, like a teddy bear. I only heard about Tauno Hannikainen. I never saw him. Schneevoigt worked mostly in America, and he was a great conductor. Jussi Jalas was quite good, too, the son-in-law of Sibelius. But over all, I would say Berglund is some kind of grand old father for Finnish conductors.

When you prepare a piece, you study the score thoroughly and imagine the sound you want. Does the sound picture ever change when you get into rehearsal? Do you hear things you hadn't imagined?

Osmo: It starts from the notes and the accents. It's one of the duties of the conductor, I think, to sort out those notes—long notes and accents—from the score and then try to understand what the composer wanted to say in his music. And then he has to find out some pictures or images that would help the orchestra to create the right kind of sound. But we don't have the scores from Beethoven or others where they write: "For these eight bars, think about the sunset. And for the next eight bars, think about the sunrise." So for the conductor the question is what kind of images are helpful, and for the players it's good if they can hear what the conductor is thinking. There are some kinds of basic settings when we rehearse. But it changes, and it changes in the concerts, too. What I enjoy so much about the Minnesota Orchestra is that they go along with those changes. In the Bruckner concert, for example, there were so many places where we exercised a freedom to do things differently, and this changed the sound immediately. There was a little bit more air in certain places. This happens when we are really listening to each other, and it happens now in every concert —points where there is some extra space or light in the music. Rehearsal is where we try to set those ideas, and then finally, if we are lucky enough, many more things happen in the concerts.

Some people hear the influence of the early-music movement in your Beethoven recordings—the quick tempos, the transparent textures. Have you listened much to the work of Nikolaus Harnoncourt and Christopher Hogwood and others?

Osmo: I've heard Harnoncourt on the radio, and I've been to some of the concerts of the early-music groups. Yes, I think it's great that we have had this opportunity to listen to the old instruments. Harnoncourt has done a great job. The romantic style of doing Beethoven, like by Karajan, was powerful. But it was as if there were some kind of silk covering the music. I have learned things from the old instrument groups, about accents, for example. This opens the range and scale of the music. It gives more options in trying to figure out what kind of accent is correct in a given place in the score, what kind of forte-pianos and so on. And it obviously tells how revolutionary a composer Beethoven was. We know that his contemporaries said, "Who can listen to this loud and ugly music?" But the romantic style of playing—Karajan and others—made it seem not revolutionary at all but merely a little bit sophisticated. Whereas now, hearing the old instruments—the old trumpets and the old oboes—we have learned a style that is more dramatic. It can be sometimes rude or it can be sometimes beautiful. But there is space for all kinds of styles.

Many symphony conductors now shy away from baroque music, or even Haydn, because they don't feel that their big, modern instrument orchestras can do the earlier music correctly. You may be an exception.

Osmo: The so-called "old" conductors might feel that they are not specialists enough compared to the people who are doing only the early music. I still work with the modern symphony orchestra, and I don't like to use the non-vibrato sound. For me, it's not an interesting sound. Yesterday I heard an excellent performance of "Messiah," with Christopher Warren-Green conducting and very good soloists. And they did many things without vibrato. But that's not my piece of cake. I would like to keep some kind of small vibrato in a performance—not this kind of slow and large vibrato. I believe that if Mozart had known the big, modern Steinway piano, he wouldn't have wanted to write only for the fortepiano. We have great things in the modern symphony orchestra. We can put old things together with the newer sounds. For me, the style of phrasing is more important than using the old instruments.

Jorja Fleezanis says that you work first toward a good strong bass sound, and then build it up vertically.

Osmo: Yes, I like this idea. The sound should be round. It starts from there, from the basses.

What was your worst experience with an orchestra?

Osmo: I don't want to name the orchestra, but there was a terrible gang in one orchestra. They played with very bad quality, but they didn't want to take anything again, that is, to rehearse anything. They complained: "No reason to do it again." It was a disaster, and I started to think, "What is wrong? Can I do my job? This is so difficult."

Then came the concert, and afterward, many people from the audience came to say hello, and my agent, too, and they all said, "This orchestra has never played so well." I was so surprised because it had been a disaster all week. Then I flew the next morning to Glasgow and the BBC Scottish Symphony. I had a rehearsal right away, and I was still thinking that something is wrong with my job. "I'm doing things wrong, and maybe I have to seriously re-think what I am doing with my life." I went to the first rehearsal—this was in 1994—

and in just one minute, maybe two minutes, I thought, "Now this is as it should be." The orchestra was ready to work. They wanted to play, and they had a good sense of humor. In just a few minutes, everything came back. I thought, "Nothing is wrong with what I am doing—well, no more than usual."

But the main thing is I enjoyed the work. It was a good atmosphere and good quality of playing. It was a joy.

Hearing your Broadway program, some expressed surprise that you displayed such an easy command of American pop and jazz idioms. Should they be surprised?

Osmo: I'm always at home when I can do that kind of music. I love listening to all kinds of, let's say, entertainment music: Benny Goodman, Miles Davis. And I played in a dance band. I feel very close to that music. And also, I feel that if I understand those rhythms, the kind that Bernstein used, the dance music, it helps me to set the rhythms in symphonic music. The rhythm guys—bass and drum—have to be very accurate. Then the guys playing melody have to be a little behind the beat, never ahead. It's like they're holding back. That's when the swing starts. The same kind of rhythms come in Mahler and others, and if we can get that music to swing where it's appropriate, it sounds good. Broadway music, symphonic music—there's no difference.

Vesa Sirén, music critic of the daily newspaper in Helsinki, has written extensively on Vänskä—and argued with him, too. "It got to the point where," Sirén recalled, "if I wrote something negative in an otherwise positive review, I would take my scores to my bedside, because there was always the chance that Osmo would call early the next morning. I would open my scores, and we would have a discussion. Sometimes he said, 'I see your point.' Other times it was, 'But you are mistaken.' I'd say, 'What?' Then I'd look at the score again. 'You won.'" (Just for the record, Osmo says that happened only once.)

The music critic in Helsinki, Vesa Sirén, says: "Osmo has this almost religious devotion to the score, which is one of Osmo's trademarks. Osmo searches for something unifying, maybe something holy—an experience of holiness in music."

Osmo: That might be an exaggeration, but not totally. I have said before that I believe that music is a gift of God to us and that I also try to be loyal to the composer. But I have never felt that the score is some kind of word of God, and then I have to find out what that word is. What I do think is that there is some kind of logic inside of music, but I don't try to connect that to God other than to say that I believe that all good music comes from God, however and whatever way one thinks about God. This gets very complicated. The religious connection might be felt more in the way that my life seems to have been planned out, though I'm not so certain about those things as I used to be. In contrast, when I was young, I thought I knew everything. I thought there was a kind of fate behind everything, and that God had a plan for my life. That's a much stronger religious connection than simply looking at scores.

When I was a teenager I believed there was this divine providence, which meant that if a person wanted to pray and to hear God, there was a plan for his or her life. I'm not the same person today as I was when I thought that, but still I cannot put it away. It has been one part of my life, and on some scale it still is. That is, there seem to be many perfect timings in my life, none of which I could have figured out myself. So where are they coming from? For instance, I didn't ask the Minnesota Orchestra to invite me. They asked me to come here, and where did they get this idea? I don't know. But things like that, they're some kind of mosaic that makes up a whole life. There are many people who have different thoughts about this. It's very sensitive and very personal. But I'm not being honest if I don't at least think about these things.

On Tour

If there is any musical aggregation that should refrain from touring the country or the world, it's a symphony orchestra. Think of moving ninety or a hundred musicians plus tons of equipment and instruments from one city to another. Then add a nightmare's worth of contingencies and hurdles that even the most careful planning cannot eliminate. Yet every year dozens of orchestras hit the road in the U.S. and Europe, and they're quite cheerful about it. They say it helps morale, improves performance, and might even sell a few CDs. At least these days, a symphony orchestra needs financial support, even for short tours.

The Minnesota Orchestra had ample funding for its European tour of 2004—$1.4 million given anonymously by its longtime patrons, Kenneth and Judy Dayton. Even so, this was a bold venture. Orchestras don't usually launch a big tour during a music director's first season. Vänskä pushed for it, nonetheless, though some people—board members and staff—suggested that they wait a year or two so that orchestra and conductor could get better acquainted. "We spoke about this," Vänskä said. "I told them, 'No, we have to do it the first season. This gives the orchestra a focus, and I like challenges.' We say in Finnish, 'Beat the wolf straight on.' Don't be scared. Go and do it."

The tour encompassed thirteen concerts, starting February 9 at Carnegie Hall, then moving on to performances in Austria, Germany, England, Scotland, and Finland. The last was a concert at Sibelius Hall in Lahti, the highly-rated new home of the orchestra that Vänskä had led to fame through recordings and tours throughout Europe and Asia. It was obvious that the concert in Lahti meant a lot to Vänskä. "The Minnesota Orchestra is quite well known in Europe," he said at the time. "People count it as one of the top American orchestras. I would like to show that I had good reason to come here, and I also want to introduce the orchestra to Sibelius Hall."

Violist Sam Bergman, who maintained a tour blog that appeared each day on the website artsjournal.com commented, "If the expectations were high for the orchestra on this tour, they were stratospheric for Osmo, who is being asked to prove his reputation on

Performing at the BBC Proms in Royal Albert Hall, London, 2006.

a global stage with an American orchestra in the very first year of his tenure with us."

The international tours made by the Minnesota Orchestra earned both orchestra and conductor ample attention and praise.

In addition there were the less publicized trips to small towns in Minnesota. The orchestra, which historically had toured the state dating back to 1907, restarted the tradition during its centennial season, 2002-2003. Vice President and General Manager Robert Neu said the orchestra has continued doing these brief tours because Vänskä believes they're important and also because the audiences are so responsive. "There will be people there who have never heard the Beethoven Seventh Symphony live or, in some cases, have never heard a professional orchestra live," he said.

The musicians like these trips, too. "My mother heard the Minneapolis Symphony in Gainsville, Ohio, in 1944," said flutist Wendy Williams. "And my grandfather, who loved music, would, I'm sure, be thrilled to know that I play in that orchestra today."

The tour began February 8 when the Minnesotans boarded a plane for New York City: 100 musicians, ten staff members, several spouses, a few children, four stage hands, a doctor, and a massage therapist. The seven tons of cargo traveled separately, as did thirty or so board members and orchestra fans, many of whom were attending only selected concerts on the tour. Reviews of the concert the following night at Carnegie Hall were mostly raves. The sentiments of Martin Bernheimer, writing in the *Financial Times*, were typical: "A romance between the conductor and his merry Midwest band seems to be in full, well-publicized form." Bernheimer complimented Vänskä on conducting the orchestra rather than the audience, and added that the orchestra returned the compliment by playing "with solidity, precision and, yes, brilliance in depth." Just about everybody was surprised and impressed with Vänskä's choice of curtain-raiser, Igor Stravinsky's seldom-heard "Symphonies of Wind Instruments." This isn't,

after all, an automatic crowd-pleaser. Nobody, it seemed, had read Vänskä's bio in the program, then put two and two together. He's a clarinet player, which means he identifies in a special way with the orchestra's wind sections. For him, this piece is home territory.

Then it was on to Vienna and a concert at the Musikverein, where, in the words of critic Kirsten Liese, "The Minnesota [Orchestra] left no doubt that it belongs in the first league," referring to the old rating of the American "Top Five" (New York, Chicago, Boston, Cleveland, Philadelphia). "Even the Viennese went out of their minds with loud bravos," wrote Liese. The orchestra and two expert singers, Ildiko Komlosi and Michele Kalmandi, performed Bartók's dark one-act opera, "Bluebeard's Castle." There was praise, too, for violinist Joshua Bell, who was the soloist for most of the tour.

Two nights later, the musicians were in Frankfurt where, again, the reviews were favorable even though the hall, the Alte Oper, was a challenge. "It felt like each section of the orchestra was playing in a separate soundproofed closet," according to Bergman. Düsseldorf would prove to be worse. "Sound seems to die six feet in front of the stage, and the loudest, most resonant chord can dissipate so quickly that you feel as if you're performing in an airlock." On landing in Berlin the afternoon after the Frankfurt concert, in preparation for a concert that night at the Philharmonie, every player in the orchestra shouted a lusty "Hey!" in response to the singing of a Russian folk tune by horn player Dave Kamminga. This is a tradition of long standing with this orchestra—a travel ritual signifying that the plane has safely hit the tarmac.

As the tour continued, it was obvious that the musicians were getting acquainted with their conductor in ways that would never happen in weekly programs at home. Bergman wrote, "Osmo is more intense than I've ever seen a conductor. He spins, jabs, and clenches his fists, and looks as if he would like to grab a sword and jump into the fray." Any orchestra tour, especially one that includes performances at the cultural capitals of Europe, puts special pressure on both conductor and orchestra. In this case, the pressure mounted because Vänskä insisted on lengthy rehearsals before many of the concerts instead of the quick brush-up rehearsals that are more common on such tours. It became clear, however, that this is a conductor who thrives under pressure. Halfway through the tour Bergman wrote, "Where Osmo's demeanor in the early rehearsals was fairly stern and even a bit domineering, we now see him cracking jokes and trading quips with the musicians during the touch-ups. Last night, when principal cello Tony Ross sought to clarify a section of the Aaron Jay Kernis piece ("Musica celestis") that had been a bit of a mess in Düsseldorf, Osmo allowed that it had been his mistake and said he would do it better next time. Tony, not convinced that he understood what we should be looking for, mentioned that he thought he'd seen an extra beat the last time around. Osmo grinned widely, turned to Tony, and loudly declared, 'Yes! There was an extra beat. Thank

you so much for pointing this out. And have I mentioned that your solo pizzicato last night was a bit loud?' The whole orchestra broke up laughing, and the offending passage went off without a hitch in the concert."

Osmo and the Minnesota Orchestra performed at London's Barbican Centre during critically-acclaimed tours in 2004 and 2009

Wendy Williams, a flutist in the orchestra, saw a side of Vänskä on the tour she hadn't known. She had her fifteen-month-old child along with her. "I would be carrying my stroller and diaper bags, and he would be the first person off the plane to grab a stroller or a diaper bag," she said. "He loves children, and that makes it a nice atmosphere in which to work, even on tour."

"Osmo was very un-diva-ish on that tour," recalled Gwen Pappas. "He traveled coach class with the rest of us, Pirkko alongside him, and he was on the buses with the orchestra.

A tour rehearsal at the Liederhalle, Stuttgart, in 2004.

Michael Pelton, Osmo's executive assistant, and I took a little side trip with him to do some interviews in London. We left a day earlier than the rest of the orchestra, and there he was, helping us with our bags when we got off the train."

By the time of the eleventh concert in Birmingham, the rigors of touring were taking their toll. "We're in the home stretch now," Bergman wrote from Birmingham. "The con-

stant travel is wearing far more heavily than it did a week ago. Add in the fact that my instrument is now truly out of adjustment from being hauled around two continents and various weather systems, and I can't claim that last night was my personal best performance of the tour." Ahead of them were just two more concerts—Glasgow and Lahti—and also the tightest scheduling of the entire journey, a plane ride out of Glasgow and then a quick bus trip to Lahti to play, as Bergman said, "the one concert that would define the entire tour forever in our memories—the one show that would make this trip a story we'd be talking about for years, rather than just another tour."

The tour party, now grown to 130 people, boarded a chartered plane at the Glasgow airport the afternoon of February 26. They were already twenty minutes late, due to slow airport security, and then, after starting out, the plane had to return to the gate to fix a fuel leak. After another fifteen-minute delay, the plane took off and arrived in Helsinki, amazingly, at 5:00 p.m., just a half-hour late. Then there was the 110 kilometer bus ride to Lahti in a snowstorm and a hoped-for arrival at 6:15, which might or might not allow time for a quick brush-up rehearsal and a hasty meal before the 7:30 concert. The concert was to be broadcast live on Finnish National Radio and Minnesota Public Radio, which meant they could not start late. The buses pulled up in front of Sibelius Hall at the appointed time.

Exactly forty minutes later, as the lobby was already filling up with audience members, the musicians were seated onstage as Vänskä walked to the podium and said, "Well, welcome to Lahti." The orchestra clapped in approval, and the rehearsal began. They went quickly through the five encores, the last of which was a traditional Finnish polka that Vänskä had arranged for this tour. That done, the musicians ran offstage to change into their concert garb. At 7:28 stagehand Dave McKoskey called for the musicians to take their places. Two minutes later the red light on the broadcast booth at the back of the hall flashed on, and concertmaster Jorja Fleezanis walked to her chair. Then to respectful applause, Vänskä appeared. He had exactly four minutes to change into his concert garb. Moving briskly to the podium, he gave the downbeat for Kernis's "Color Wheel," a challenge for both orchestra and audience. Joshua Bell then delivered an especially high-energy account of the work he had been playing admirably all through the tour, the Tchaikovsky Violin Concerto, drawing cheers from the audience at the end.

During intermission, while the orchestra's personnel manager, Julie Haight-Curran, attended to a violinist suffering from food poisoning, Principal Cello Tony Ross ran around backstage talking to other musicians about a surprise that Vänskä, who would turn fifty-one at midnight, wasn't to know about. The concert resumed with "Romeo and Juliet," during which, as Bergman said, "Everyone was playing with their foot hard on the accelerator. Whereas some of our recent shows had suffered from the brutal fatigue we were all feeling, this performance had the air of a football team driving for the goal line with the clock down under two minutes."

When the music ended, there was five seconds of silence—a typical Finnish reaction—and then the hall exploded with applause. Vänskä returned to the stage five times for bows, and then launched into the first encore, a Prokofiev march. Speaking first in Finnish, then in English, Vänskä dedicated the second encore, Minnesota composer Steve Heitzeg's "Wounded Fields," to Kenneth Dayton, the orchestra's longtime patron who, with his wife, had funded the tour just before he died. Dayton's widow, Judy, was seated in the audience. It was in response to the final encore, Vänskä's Finnish polka, that the audience abandoned all reserve. As Bergman recalled it, "The place went crazy. The audience roared with laughter, and immediately began enthusiastically clapping along in time. When we reached the last line of the piece, where the music stops dead, and the clarinet plays a soft cuckoo call before the orchestra buries him in a fortissimo resolution, the roomful of Finns hooted and cackled and cheered like nothing we'd ever heard. I must confess, I felt tears come to my eyes as Osmo brought us to our feet, and I was far from the only one."

When he arrived in Lahti in 2004, Osmo was warmly greeted by Lilja, his daughter Tytti's dog. He says, "I love dogs, but because of my travel schedule, there is no chance to have a dog now."

The improvised version of "Happy Birthday," cued by Ross when Vänskä was looking elsewhere onstage, was the final gesture in a long evening. The audience cheered one last time, Vänskä bowed again and took Fleezanis's arm and led her off stage, indicating that the music had finally come to an end. Bergman wrote, "Most tours end with a whimper, not a bang. In Lahti, we got a chance to end our trip on the highest of high notes, with a performance that probably meant more to Osmo than all the other concerts combined. The energy that was mustered for this show was something I've never seen in a professional orchestra, and to be a part of such an evening is too profound an experience to sum up in any sort of clinical style."

Orchestra Hall Diary

A week in the life of the Minnesota Orchestra as they prepare the program for the weekend concerts: Johann Sebastian Bach's Brandenburg Concerto No. 3, Ludwig van Beethoven's Piano Concerto No. 4 in G, Johannes Brahms' Symphony No. 1 in C minor.

Monday

At 9:15 a.m. Michael Pelton, Osmo's executive assistant, sits at his desk staring at the computer screen in front of him. He had arrived at 8:45. In accordance with his morning routine, he made coffee and straightened Osmo's studio.

Pelton works closely with the music director, keeping his schedule, arranging his travel, running errands, lining up tickets for hockey games, giving order to his life. Pelton joined the orchestra staff in 1995. He says, "Osmo is very grounded. He listens intently. When he says something, there's thought behind it. It's never a flippant answer. And I've never seen him have an explosion of anger. If something upset him in a rehearsal, he'll say to the individual, 'May I see you?' He'll remove the emotion behind it, then deal with it behind a closed door. He's an extremely patient person."

Jorja Fleezanis, concertmaster, enters hurriedly at 9:45. Her studio is next to Osmo's. Eric Sjostrom, associate principal librarian, goes into Jorja's studio, giving her parts for a later performance. The assistant personnel manager enters

with the rehearsal order, a listing of the day's rehearsal schedule, which carefully adheres to the union contract. On this day, a break, if it occurs, must begin between 10:40 and 11:30 a.m. Without a break, the rehearsal must end at 11:50 (as opposed to 12:30).

The pace backstage picks up. At 9:55 personnel manager Julie Haight-Curran, who has been with the orchestra since 1979, announces a five-minute call over the loud speaker. Osmo enters right at that moment, wearing a sporty dark-brown coat, khaki pants, and soft leather shoes.

Haight-Curran stands by the stage door. She says, "We're on the path of a missing violinist." The violinist had been delayed in a return flight from somewhere. "Usually they're good about calling us," she said. There had been no call. The other problem she had to deal with that morning was a sick cellist, which necessitated re-seating the cello section.

Osmo says he spent much of the weekend working on the Brahms Symphony No. 1, which he is about to rehearse. "I have not done Brahms the past few years, and that was on purpose," he says. "These are pieces that are done so often, and I have thought that I need some time to find my own way to do them. I don't want to play them the way they are always played and in ways that I have heard other people do them.

"They have played it here so many times, just last summer, for instance. It's not a question about the orchestra. It's really a matter of their learning how I will do it. I try to go a little toward Beethoven."

Having shed his coat and stripped down to one of his apparently endless supply of t-shirts, Osmo walks onstage at exactly 10:00 a.m., his scores in hand, the ninety-six musicians of the orchestra all in place. He mounts the podium and tells a story about a bandage that came loose during the Saturday concert. A few weeks earlier he had fallen while jogging and had been wearing a large bandage on his arm ever since. On Saturday night he was moving his arms so vigorously at the podium, and sweating so much, that the bandage flew off and landed on his music stand.

The story earns a vigorous chuckle, and Osmo launches into the Brahms. He gets about sixty bars into the first movement, then stops and gives detailed instructions. Later at bar 273 he says to the strings, "The important thing there is color; don't play too softly." He tells Peter Kogan not to play the extra timpani parts that are so often added but aren't in the score. Osmo's gestures are energetic. His whole body is engaged. He often stands up from his stool. A frequent gesture: left hand held stiff at a low angle, the hand shaking. Another: a mid-level 180-degree swipe, left to right, both hands holding the baton. In the third movement he addresses the second violins: "Don't play too fast there. Don't get too excited." To signal a stop he claps his hands. Osmo calls for a break at 11:20.

Rehearsal resumes at 11:40. At 12:29, on a signal from the assistant personnel manager standing by the stage door, he stops and calls a one-hour break.

At 12:35, he greets Yevgeny Sudbin at the door of his office. They embrace. Sudbin, tall, slim, wearing glasses and displaying a shy smile, enters carrying his score, looking like a serious graduate student coming for advice on his term paper. But this is a pianist with a major career already in ascendance and a half-dozen significant recordings under his belt. His performance here the prior season of Beethoven's "Emperor" Concerto with Osmo conducting had been widely acclaimed. "Where did you fly from?" asks Osmo. Sudbin: "New York—London, actually." Sudbin, 28 and recently married, lives just outside London.

He goes immediately to the piano, and Osmo takes a chair close by. He tells Sudbin a story. He was rehearsing this concerto in Lahti with another Russian pianist, Lazar Berman. "He demanded that I conduct the beginning, which is, of course, a solo part. I said, 'No, that's your part.' He said,

'No, it should be part of the whole performance. You have to conduct, and I play as you are conducting.' I said, 'Really, it looks stupid for me to do it.' He wouldn't give up. So when we did it that way, he was so nervous, for some reason, that he pushed the wrong pedal, and it came out this big staccato."

Sudbin starts with the famous opening chords. Osmo stops him after the first phrase is finished and suggests keeping it more in tempo, that is, with less of the stretched phrases favored by many pianists. Sudbin obliges, taking it again, tighter. They continue, stopping only occasionally to coordinate orchestra and solo parts. Osmo, the score in his lap, sings some of the orchestra part as Sudbin plays. Then he asks that they go back to the beginning. "Try it again, almost in tempo," he says, adding, "There is a line between being too mechanical and too personal." Sudbin does it fairly strictly this time but with tapered dynamics and an enveloping warmth of tone. Osmo smiles. "I like it very, very much," he says.

The sessions with Sudbin went well: a real collaboration, a sharing of ideas. "I cannot push a soloist far," Osmo said. "They have to play the piece. I can only give my ideas, but then they have to make the decisions because it's their responsibility finally. So it's very seldom that I have to argue with anyone. I have my own part in the program without the soloist, and that's my chance to do as I like. Then when I have a soloist, I might give some ideas, but if they want to go one way, then I have to follow them. And it's sometimes a professional challenge to go in a different style. So I think it's unfair to the soloist, if we invite him here and then I ask him to change everything. When I have given my ideas, I then step back. They heard it, but it's their business to do it or not. But also when we are here working on a piece, I try to learn as much as possible their way of doing it so that I can put my musical parts to the same interpretation that they are doing, because it would be bad if there were two interpretations: the soloist going one way, and then I come with the orchestra

and go a totally different way. That doesn't work. It must be one interpretation, and we try to come together."

At 1:30 they are both onstage with the orchestra. Osmo conducts 200 measures, then calls for basses and cellos to play the passage at bar 89 more softly, and has them do it again. Then he goes back to bar 10, asking that a sforzando, a strong accent, in the strings be longer. Generally, his manner is collegial and warmly approving when things go right. All told, he must have said "Thank you" fifty times this day during rehearsal. But he can also be harsh. At one point he addresses the basses: "Someone is playing without ears, playing ahead of the others, so it's difficult, especially when the soloist is playing so clearly. So open your ears or at least your eyes—maybe both."

At 2:55 Osmo is rehearsing the remaining work on the program, Johann Sebastian Bach's Brandenburg Concerto No. 3 in a version that will be quite new to most listeners. Bach rescored the first movement of

Michael Sutton, violin

"This is a different style of Brahms. We're used to sustaining the notes. Even if you have a dot over the note, it's held longer than usual. Whereas Osmo's having us taper the notes, hitting them and then letting the sound fade away. That's new to me.

"Actually the business of hitting a note, then going away, is an idea from the classical period. It's kind of a throwback, and that's legitimate—Brahms was always looking back to Mozart. Whereas I've always been told to cling to the notes like there's no tomorrow. I assume that Osmo's doing this because he wants other parts of the score to be heard more clearly. The other thing is, he's sticking very close to the score. Where, traditionally, we might take more time with something and stretch things out, he goes right through it because he sees that that's what Brahms wrote. A lot of those things we're used to adding, he takes out. When Osmo's conducting, I always come to a first rehearsal with a big eraser at the end of my pencil, because there's a lot of stuff on my score that's going to go."

this piece some ten years after composing the Brandenburgs, adding five wind players to make up the Sinfonia of the sacred Cantata No. 174. Osmo is also adding some string players, bringing the ensemble up to about thirty.

$\mathcal{W}$illiam Schrickel, acting associate principal bass

A thirty-two-year veteran of this orchestra, William Schrickel approves of Osmo's addition of extra strings in the Bach. "I'm used to hearing it with just ten players and a harpsichord. But it's a heavy piece if you do it that way. The counterpoint is hard to hear, especially in this hall."

As for the Brahms: "I personally have room for a lot of different approaches to that symphony. I've read analyses of the use of vibrato during Brahms' time, and they make a convincing case that it wasn't common back then to play with this big, rich sound, which is the way we did it last summer with Andrew Litton. That sort of version is what a lot of us grew up listening to. But I don't think that big, tubby sound was what Brahms expected to hear."

During the last part of the rehearsal, he makes extensive adjustments in balance and, at one point, asks for more sound from the English horn. "Marni [J. Hougham], make those two quarter notes very loud. Show that you have something there to do." He apologizes at one point: "Maybe I had my downbeat in the wrong place."

Tuesday

"The string players have been taking long, accented notes in Brahms," Osmo says. "They come at different times—different from the winds." He sings an example: "DE-duh, DE-duh. My understanding of accents is not only how to start the note but how to end it. So for me, an accent is (he sings) 'BAHHHhhhh.'" His voice fades away, as in a diminuendo. "Instead of 'BAHHHHH!' In fact, I think it should always be a diminuendo, even though it's very short. The result is it gives more space for other things." He grabs

his score off his desk and points to a passage in the first movement where the accent actually comes from the woodwinds, but the note is covered if the strings do a fully-sustained note. "The whole thing is more transparent this way. This comes very much from Beethoven and the Vienna classical period. Sustaining a long note isn't very interesting, especially for the brass. If they do that, no one can hear anything else." He demonstates—"POW!"—then sings a series of descending pitches.

"In Mahler, for example, those long notes also have rhythmical properties. If there is an accent and we play it, it gives more this kind of [loudly] 'TAHN-THAN' instead of [softly] 'rah-rah-rah.' Actually, this instrument is a good example of [the value of] not sustaining the note. Every note marked 'piano' is always going away, and that helps make greater transparency and balance. And it also brings to the music this kind of swing. It goes without pushing it.

"The discipline is so good with this orchestra. Whatever I ask, they are quick to do it. When we started yesterday I told them that I know they know the piece. I heard them last summer when they played it with Andrew Litton. So I told them that the only thing we have to do is try to put my ideas in there, but that we don't need to waste time just playing it. We'll just try to move those things that I would like to change, and then it's ready to go.

"Also, I hold tempos fairly firm. I try to stay as loyal as possible to the composer. That's one starting point. I believe that if the composer wanted to have a ritenuto or some addition, he would write it that way. So when I hear things that are done without orders from the composer, then I put a question mark there. I think it's more obvious when we go to older music, to Viennese classical music, that the style is more stable. You don't make a lot of ritardandos and ritenutos. Whereas, when you come to romantic music, conductors do a lot of things. They stop and they go and they pause.

That's an interesting area. I know that if we don't do anything there, if we don't breathe faster and slower, then the music might become too mechanical. But where is the line when we are doing too many of our own things and we don't follow the composer? That's some kind of secret in music, and there's no perfect answer to it. I'm not the teacher to anyone else, but my own idea of music-making is that I need to be convinced that what I am doing is coming from the composer. It must be Brahms' First Symphony, not Vänskä's version of the Brahms First Symphony. The problem is that when people are used to those stops and a lot of rhythmical freedom, they feel insecure when someone asks them to keep up the tempo. There are some, I'm sure, who criticize me, saying that I don't do enough of what they consider music. But there are others who feel that this is the way it should be. That's the thing in music. There are no final truths."

One violinist described Vänskä's Brahms as "cold" and "mechanical" and lacking lyricism. Another violinist offered a different view. He especially liked the unrelenting pacing of the finale. He told Vänskä, "I have been waiting for thirty years to do that passage—the horn-call—in tempo. You are the first to do it."

Osmo comments, "The Bach Concerto went very smoothly. And it's a new thing: The first movement is a bigger orchestration than what is normally used these days. I didn't stop. That's the way it should be. I stop in rehearsal only if things aren't going in the way I like. I know, for example, that the next time we play Brahms First Symphony together, they will remember what I have asked them, and then I don't need to stop. We played the Beethoven Seventh Symphony last summer, a piece we had recorded, and so in rehearsal I said hardly anything. For example, I didn't stop so often in rehearsing the concerto because the players are used to playing Beethoven in the way I have asked. So the style is there, and because of that I don't need to stop. Also, when there is a soloist, many things

are coming out of his playing. He plays something, and then the orchestra understands that's the way to phrase it. The soloist plays, and we try to follow him. So there's no reason to stop, because they can hear it."

"In the two rehearsals tomorrow some parts will be exactly as I asked. Some will be a little like compromising. So I have to take care that these ideas are still there and that everyone is playing in this one way. It could be tomorrow that some people are still playing in the old style while others are playing what I asked them to do. Then I have to control that, so that we have only one interpretation, not two. But it will be shorter tomorrow. We won't need so much time. I always work harder in the first rehearsal. If I lose that momentum, then I cannot change it anymore. If we play one way and I don't say anything, then people will believe that's how we're going to play it, and I can't come back again and try to change things. So I have to show in the beginning that this is the way to do it. In other words, tomorrow will be some kind of follow-up."

Kari Sundström, trombone

"Osmo works on details, but he's interested in the big picture, too. That's what's great about him. There is a nice balance with him, and he's also collaborative. I like that. . . . He's a humble personality. He comes across as a human being. He makes mistakes; we make mistakes. There aren't a lot of conductors who will admit to a mistake.

"There's always a delicate balance—the chemistry between a conductor and the hundred or so players in an orchestra. Everything about Osmo is about work. When he's putting a piece together in rehearsal, it's slow, meticulous work, just like his career moved slowly and meticulously. Osmo follows the score religiously. He's after rhythmical precision and balance and extreme dynamics. That's why his recordings and his concerts are so exciting. It's a problem, you know, to play in this hall, a problem to play together. He has made the ensemble much tighter."

Wednesday

Julie Haight-Curran says that the missing violinist was in Nashville. "He got the schedule fouled up. He was horrified to find out he was supposed to be here. But he's here now."

𝒥onathan Magness, associate principal second violin

Jonathan Magness listened to a recording of the Brahms First Symphony just to familiarize himself with the piece, though he has played it any number of times. The recording "was Karajan—very traditional. Whereas the way Osmo is doing it, you hear a lot of other things you don't normally hear. It's a lighter approach. It is not that it is more difficult to do this way. It's a little more classical. That's not how I've ever played it before."

In a lot of repertoire, Osmo's approach works well, he says. "Sometimes it's a little complicated, and sometimes I feel that if you micro-manage every phrase, it comes out that way. On the other hand, I have tremendous respect for Osmo and his musicianship. I don't agree with everything he does, but most of what he's done has been great, especially his Beethoven."

It could have been worse; it could have been a concert. "If somebody's not here for a concert, and there's an empty chair, I'll call the stage door: 'Have you seen so-and-so come in?' And if they're not there, it's, like, 'Whoa!' Because you do want to convey to the audience that everything's just hunky-dory.'" She laughs. "It happens. Somebody reads the schedule wrong, thinking a certain Thursday is a Coffee Concert day instead of a rehearsal day. We just remind people to look at their schedules. Then there are musicians getting sick during a concert." This happens more often on tours, during which, as she says, "Musicians don't eat right or sleep right. I remember a musician saying during intermission he didn't feel well. But he decided to play anyway. Well, he played about ten bars and then had to run off stage. We had a waste basket ready."

Osmo steps to the podium, says one word to the orchestra, "Brahms," and gives a downbeat. He stops right before the first Allegro, and asks for more articulation from the timpani on the first bar. Then, on bar 9, he asks for less force. "It's not a sforzando," he says. Then he underlines a diminuendo at 12. Later: "I don't hear the woodwinds at 84, but I don't know if there's anything we can do about that because it's quite heavy there. But try." On that same page he asks the strings to pull away from some accented notes—the kind of fade-away on sustained notes that he's asking for throughout this symphony. "I like very much the beginning. Thank you for that," he says. "Basses, thank you for the articulation. Now I can hear it, almost. Give all that you have there."

"Cellos." Osmo says, "Let's go away from the long notes." He sings it. "Don't sustain too much." The same for the horns. At one point he asks for a feeling of frustration in the music—evoking the Minnesota Twins, who lost the night before. He works the final chord, building it up from C to E, with just the woodwinds playing. "It's sharp," he says. Eventually, it's perfect.

He starts on the second movement, shaping the opening phrase. He sings it. "Could it be like one simple flower that you give to your mother, nothing plastic? Not too much art. That's a beautiful pianissimo you do in the third bar. Basses, that's really beautiful. But don't do so much ritenuto on B-natural. Just play the last note longer. It will be even better, to my taste at least. It may be strange. Strings, fourth bar of D. It's very close. What I want you to do is this Hungarian style." He sings a kind of syrupy, sentimental line. To the strings right before B: "If you could take it a little more backstage. It sounds like someone is making too much drama." He sings again in an exaggerated manner.

At 1:55 Osmo and Sudbin are conferring onstage. He turns to the orchestra. He asks them to try piano on a passage, "But don't write it down yet." He asks for very clear articulation from the strings in the opening bars of the finale.

Osmo brings the concerto rehearsal to a stop. "I think this is OK. We can survive with this." He starts the Bach with the brief continuo solo that separates the two movements. Later: "Can we start this again and keep it on the lighter side?" He stops at 3:13.

Thursday

At the 11:00 a.m. Coffee Concert, Sudbin is in fine form. The passagework in this most subtle and potentially most moving of Beethoven's piano concertos is delivered with unerring precision and elegant legato, and yet the phrasing seems entirely natural. The sound is warm and multi-colored, the slow movement is properly meditative, and the first-movement cadenza (the longer of the two that Beethoven provided) carries the hoped-for feeling of improvisation. When it is over, the audience erupts into applause and a standing ovation.

Osmo's Brahms piece is really a different take on this composer, and those differences are easier to hear this morning than they were in the stop-and-start rehearsals the past two days. It's partly Osmo's accents—pulling back on sustained notes. It is most clear in the final measures of the first movement, especially in the strings, and throughout the exquisitely phrased slow movement. It does two things: it takes some of the thickness out of Brahms' orchestration, which so often sounds like molasses, and it shines a light on whatever else is going on in the score at that moment, which in Brahms' case is usually a lot. As Osmo contends, this takes us back to the performance practice of Brahms' own time, or back even further to Beethoven. We don't really know what orchestras sounded like 130 years ago. Osmo held the tempos firmly though not rigidly, especially in the outer movements and most notably right before the aforementioned brass chorale, where most conductors make a big ritard and a pause. Osmo charged right through it, like a high-speed bullet train. It's more exciting that way. Nothing

is lost except ponderousness. And we can only guess that that's the way Brahms wanted it, too.

What would Bach have thought about this version of his Brandenburg Concerto No. 3? For the first movement Osmo used an orchestration Bach himself did of the same music for his Cantata No. 174, adding woodwinds and brass. Osmo also beefed up the string section so that about thirty musicians were involved. For the second (and final) movement he used the string ensemble scoring to which we are accustomed. The first movement sounded strange. The wind parts added spice to the harmonies, but it was all too thick, a trifle murky. A lively concert in any case.

Friday

The Friday night concert begins the same way the Coffee Concert began, with a spontaneous gesture of affection from the audience toward the concertmaster of twenty seasons, Jorja Fleezanis, as she takes her regular seat to the left of the podium. Fleezanis announced a week earlier that she

Manny Laureano, principal trumpet

Manny Laureano plays a modified corno da caccia, a baroque hunting horn, in the Brandenburg Concerto. "We so infrequently get to play Bach that I'll jump at the chance to play that music under any circumstances," he says.

On Osmo's Brahms style, Laureano says, "Osmo might be right," meaning that this approach might be more historically accurate. On the other hand, Manny is less impressed with Osmo's firmly-held tempos, especially at that point in the finale right before the brass chorale. "I had never heard it done the way that Osmo's doing it. But I'll tell you, Osmo's had so much success in so many other areas of music that he's earned the right to go ahead and be different, and the reason I'll buy into it is that I don't think he's doing it just to be different. That sort of thing drives me nuts. But I think he has an approach, and he'll try it, and I'll see that approach evolve during the week in rehearsals."

Jorja Fleezanis, concertmaster

Jorja Fleezanis sees Osmo's approach to Brahms as going back to a more classical style. "The performance tradition in this repertory by now is the result of Klemperer, Furtwängler, Bernstein, Karajan. To find your own niche in this repertory, you have to just shut everything out and say, 'How do I see this music, and what stylistic frame do I want to put it in?' He's doing this more like Beethoven than like a more vitamin-ized, sostenuto style that has become the foundation of twentieth-century playing.

"So often, people's idea of Brahms is a place to self-indulge. It's what Brahms does to us. We want to be there for these emotional needs—the needs he seems to raise in us. Osmo's more restrained. He wants the emotion, but he doesn't want to show it in any indulgent way. He doesn't go to that high-cholesterol level. I know that that can seem frustrating for string players. It's this thing of getting in and coddling things. That's something that many of us were raised to do. Some of it doesn't feel comfortable yet to me. It's not in our blood. We haven't had enough time to explore it."

would be leaving to become professor of music at the Indiana University Jacobs School of Music. The applause went on and on, and Fleezanis, who has become a vital member of this orchestra and this community, seemed genuinely moved by the audience's acknowledgment. It is the kind of affection a musician doesn't earn quickly, and for many concertgoers it surely will be hard to imagine anyone else sitting in that chair—or anyone else in the position who possesses her qualities of musicianship, intense dedication, and communicative flair.

Perhaps this extra swell of emotion from the audience gave the playing Friday night a boost. In most regards, it was a better performance than the one Thursday morning. The Bach was more genial in tone, more relaxed than it had been. The woodwinds in the first movement seemed less out-of-place. This time they sound like raindrops falling right on the mark, and the whole piece, but especially the first movement, sounds less cluttered.

Sudbin's Beethoven is a little more unbuttoned this time around. He really tears into the middle section of the first-movement cadenza, much the way one imagines Beethoven played it. His passagework in the outer movements is even lighter than before, the notes like pearls on a string, and Vänskä's tempo in the finale has speeded up a bit.

The Brahms was good before. It's better the second time. For one thing, the players are more consistent in delivering the kind of tapered phrasing of sustained notes that Vänskä worked on so hard during rehearsal. There is light shining through the music this time, and Vänskä's tempos seem even more shrewd in this performance. He gets a true andante in the second movement. It's a little bit faster than it was Thursday morning. The audience loves it.

Saturday

The Saturday performance was the most impressive of the three this week. The playing was alert yet relaxed. It was as if the musicians now lived inside the music. Knots in the Bach had been unraveled. Sudbin was marvelous in the Beethoven, offering playing that mixed delicate nuance with real strength and forward motion. The Brahms came together beautifully, a highly individual reading that was at the same time consistent and musically scrupulous. Small details, such as the tapering of the notes in the octave theme in the trio of the third movement, seemed, rather than fussy, to be the way those notes should go, only no one else before had taken the pains to do it. And yet the whole sweep of the work—the big picture—was never lost.

Behind the Scenes

A week at Orchestra Hall, talking to people, going to rehearsals and concerts, and observing what happens in this strange world makes clear that there are many activities and people supporting and contributing to the conductor's success.

Planning Programs

Who's really responsible for the orchestra's programs? Is it the music director or a committee? "It's a pooling of ideas," said Robert Neu, vice president and general manager. "But the music director's preferences are what rules the roost. What he wants to program is paramount. Everything else is a suggestion. I mean, Osmo's the one at the podium who has to make it work. He's also the one who has the overview of the whole season. Certainly guest conductors and soloists will come with things they would like to do. I'll say, 'Here's what they're suggesting. What do you think?' He might say, 'That sounds great,' but not always. He might say, 'That's a piece I really want to do the season after.'"

Certain ideas obviously come from Osmo—the Nielsen symphonies that he programmed during his first two seasons. It made sense: they're under-appreciated works that Osmo had performed and recorded just a few years earlier with the BBC Scottish Symphony Orchestra. But what of something like the festival in January 2009, devoted to the music of Leonard Bernstein? It was judicious mix of the familiar and unfamiliar culminating in staged performances of Bernstein's "Mass," a controversial oratorio from 1971. Given the diversity of the festival, surely this was the product of a brainstorming session rather than the work of one person. "In planning a season, we always look at what the significant anniversaries are, and 2008 was Bernstein's ninetieth birthday. So that was the jumping-off point," said Neu. "Osmo's very interested in American music, and the Bernstein things he had done in the past he really liked. So then we just started coming up with ideas.

Osmo at home.

"The point is, when you work with the best collaborators, as is the case here, at the end of the day you don't remember whose idea it was."

Jorja Fleezanis, concertmaster

She was the Minnesota Orchestra's first female concertmaster and only the second woman in the United States to hold the top spot in a major orchestra. "As concertmaster she is the conductor's first lieutenant. She develops the ensemble's particular sound and makes technical decisions for the section about how to negotiate the bow through the passages" (Kim Ode, *Star Tribune*, June 13, 2009). Under her guidance and encouragement, the strings of this orchestra took on a color and vibrancy never heard here before. In the Vänskä years to those qualities were added a precision of ensemble and a rhythmic exactitude that few orchestras today can match.

Osmo and the Minnesota Orchestra at the Lake Harriet Bandshell in Minneapolis.

As a soloist, she played the memorable premieres of the Adams Violin Concerto in 1994 and the Tavener "Ikon of Eros," both composed for her, along with numerous other large-scale, often lesser-known works. She was busy as a teacher at Hamline University. She was also busy throughout these years at the University of Minnesota School of Music, and she was active in the Twin Cities as a chamber music player.

Paul Gunther, principal librarian

Paul Gunther is responsible for lining up scores and parts for the hundred or so works that the orchestra plays in an average season and for maintaining the orchestra's own library of some 5,000 scores. For him a bad week is "the last-minute surprise. We get word on programming pretty far in advance, which means we can anticipate potential problems. It's the surprises that are trouble, like a guest conductor who thinks he told us one thing and actually told us another. Last year, for a guest violinist, someone noticed we had the wrong Mendelssohn violin concerto. We thought it was the obscure one, D-minor, I think it is. Someone said 'You know, it's not likely that this visiting artist, here for the first time, is going to do this obscure concerto." He contacted the violinist's manager, who said, "Of course it's the famous one." "That would have been unpleasant if we had put out the parts for the wrong concerto," Gunther said.

On occasion, with little time to spare before rehearsals were scheduled to begin, either Gunther or Eric Sjostrom, associate principal librarian, has had to fly to New York to pick up parts. Sjostrom recalls a sudden trip to New York during a Good Friday weekend in the De Waart era to get parts for the Rachmaninoff-Respighi "Tableaux." The publisher's office closed early on that Friday, so they couldn't get through to them that day. They needed the parts on Tuesday, so Sjostrom flew to New York on Sunday. Early Monday morning he called Mark Wilson at the publisher's office. "I said, 'Hi, Mark. This is Eric Sjostrom. I need the parts for the Rachmaninoff-Respighi "Tableaux."' He said, 'OK, we'll send it to you.' I said, 'No, you don't understand. I'm in the lobby. I need it now.' He said, 'Oh, my God.'" Sjostrom got the parts and took off from La Guardia in just a few hours.

Gunther says, "I would say this library has had triple-A ratings with every music director we've had. These guys have a lot of responsibility on their shoulders. So if they want something soon, they really want it soon. The typical library quandary is when there's a lot that has to be done, either before or during rehearsal, and that's when the conductor asks for something. We can't say, 'Can you wait?'"

Vänskä's scores sit on a nearby shelf—all except his Sibelius scores, which he keeps at home. "With Osmo, we do a lot of e-mail back and forth on things he needs or things I need. With him, there are no impediments. He's very clear about what he wants."

Michael Pelton, executive assistant to Osmo Vänskä

As executive assistant to the music director, Michael Pelton manages the administrative support and daily logistics of Osmo Vänskä's office. He coordinates short- and long-term calendars for Osmo, provides personal support, and manages his domestic and international travel. Pelton manages and prioritizes the music director's media, fundraising, and community activities, organizes and crafts communications as needed, and serves as the music director's liaison to all Minnesota Orchestra constituents.

He operates within the artistic planning department, and many projects and daily responsibilities involve a large planning dimension for future seasons. Pelton communicates on a regular basis with Osmo's various constituents domestically and internationally for the purposes of long-range scheduling and planning with various orchestras. In developing continuing relationships with guest conductors and artists, Pelton is also responsible for the numerous artists engaged by the orchestra, working with artist management agencies regarding the execution of negotiated contracts—travel, accommodations, artist itineraries, and work visa arrangements.

Pelton provides the music director with daily updates wherever his location on the globe and serves as a close confidant.

Orchestra Hall Acoustics

Saturday night audiences at Orchestra Hall are more energetic than those earlier in the week. They haven't worked all day long. Audience behavior has improved since Orchestra Hall opened in 1974. Back then, people in the Twin Cities weren't used to hearing orchestra music in a hall with the kind of bright acoustics that magnifies the sound of coughing, sneezing, snoring, program rattling, whispering, foot tapping, and all the other noises that humans make and, most of the time, seem not to notice. Northrop Auditorium, where the orchestra used to play, was fairly dead acoustically. A cough got swallowed up in the aural muck, whereas at Orchestra Hall coughing was like little explosions going on constantly during the concerts, often drowning out the music, especially the soft passages. That may be why Vänskä's predecessors didn't work to the extent that he has on getting the orchestra to play softly. They figured the audience wouldn't hear it anyway.

On a typical concert day, nothing is scheduled for Osmo after 3:00 p.m He has time to be home and he usually takes a nap—twenty or thirty minutes maximum—before he leaves for a concert. Or he spends thirty minutes playing his clarinet. For an 8:00 concert, he will show up at 7:40 or 7:45. He gets dressed and sits down and goes over his scores, usually with his metronome. Post-concert, he goes home and usually takes a sauna—this after sweating for two hours on the podium. Normally he needs an hour to decompress.

The turning point may have been that legendary night in the late 1970s when Neville Marriner stopped the music, turned around, and chastised the audience for the volley of coughing and wheezing and throat clearing that had reached some kind of cataclysm that night—the audience strumming its catarrh, as the old joke goes. Some in the audience applauded Marriner's reprimand. Others reached for a handkerchief.

It's gotten better in the ensuing years. Vänskä has gone even further—training the audience to hold their applause at the end of a piece until he has lowered his arms to his sides. And he obviously doesn't like applause between the movements of a symphony or concerto. If he acknowledges such wayward applause at all, he does it with a quick turn-around and a nod of the head.

Vänskä has made other improvements: putting the brass players on risers, for instance, which means the trumpets and trombones do not blow out the ear drums of the violists, at least not to the degree that was the case when they were on the same level as the now only partially deaf violists. He also insisted on putting the first and second violins opposite one another on either side of the podium, as was the format in Mozart's time and at least up through the days of Mahler. Other conductors had done this here from time to time, but Vänskä has wisely made it permanent, unless a certain score demands some other kind of seating. This arrangement helps clarify music in which first and second violins are treated antiphonally and also aids in realizing one of Vänskä's obsessions: bringing out the inner voices of a score, at least where it relates to the strings.

Other things he can't really fix, like the fact that the musicians still have trouble hearing each other onstage. Some years back, with the permission of Cyril Harris who designed

Osmo with Andrew Litton, artistic director for Sommerfest.

the hall's acoustics, one row of the big white cubes that adorn the ceiling and back wall was removed—the one closest to the floor of the stage. This may have helped. Harris, incidentally, said at the time that the onstage cubes, which were thought to be so important to the hall's acoustics, actually had no effect on the sound at all. They were there merely for decoration. It was the rectangular shape of the hall that was the chief factor in acoustics, he said.

Guest Artist

Jean-Yves Thibaudet was stressed out when he arrived in Minneapolis in late May 2008. His schedule had been hectic. The prior week he had played the Camille Saint-Saëns Piano Concerto No. 5 in Spain and then the two George Gershwin concertos—the "Rhapsody in Blue" and the Concerto in F—elsewhere. On top of that, he had spent months learning a new concerto that he was scheduled to premiere the following week. And now here he was with the Minnesota Orchestra about to rehearse a difficult work that he hadn't played in a decade, Rachmaninoff's Rhapsody on a Theme of Paganini. Even though the agreement to play the Rachmaninoff had been on the books for more than two years, he had asked Osmo some weeks earlier if he could substitute "one of the concertos that is easier for me," like the Ravel or the Grieg concerto. "I tried that, but it didn't work," Thibaudet laughed. Osmo said he needed the Rachmaninoff.

"You know, I understand and respect his point," said Thibaudet. "He could have said, 'It doesn't matter. Do whatever you want.' But Osmo is someone who does real programs. He thinks about them thoroughly. A change would have ruined his program."

When Thibaudet entered Vänskä's office on a Tuesday afternoon to go over the Rachmaninoff, they walked over to the piano. "I haven't played this since 1997 or 1998," he said as he sat down at the piano. They started through the piece. Vänskä sat in a chair nearby reading the score. At Variations 13 and 18 (the famous one), he sang the melody while beating time. They moved quickly through all twenty-four variations, seldom stopping.

Thibaudet seemed to have no trouble with any of it. "Memory was actually my biggest concern," he said afterward. "If you're playing a piece all the time, the reflexes are there, but when you haven't played something for many years, it's hard work bringing it back."

They've worked together often, Thibaudet and Vänskä. "Osmo's a fantastic accompanist," he said, "which means he really listens, and he's completely flexible. He doesn't say, the way older conductors like Karajan used to, 'This is my way. You must do it.' You have no idea how many conductors are like that. Osmo, on the other hand, is a real player. It's like riding in a Rolls Royce. He makes you feel comfortable."

Thibaudet has considerable history with this orchestra and its various music directors. "This orchestra is playing wonderfully. People talk about the Philadelphia Orchestra, but I keep telling them when I'm traveling, 'Be aware that in some other cities there are orchestras that are just about at that level: Minnesota, Atlanta. There are so many of them. It's unbelievable. That's something so rich in this country."

An Orchestra Builder

By the fall of 2008, the start of Vänskä's sixth season at the helm of the Minnesota Orchestra, the area around Orchestra Hall in downtown Minneapolis could have been called Vänskä Country. It wasn't just that the conductor's face appeared on the front of the hall in a photograph twenty feet high. The potentially combative relationship between conductor and orchestra so often described as a marriage had been a success.

The European tour of 2004 had earned mostly rave reviews, as had the return visit two years later, an excursion to a half-dozen important European music festivals and a third trip to Europe which took place in February 2009. The first release in the Beethoven symphonies set—Symphonies No. 4 and 5—had been called "the modern Beethoven recording par excellence" (*Financial Times*). In 2007 a critic of the *New York Times* asserted that the Minnesota Orchestra was "if not the best American orchestra, at least the most important." Not only was the orchestra playing night after night with a new-found precision and purpose, but the musicians had come to like their new music director while respecting him as well.

Vänskä had his detractors, to be sure. Some thought he demanded too much or was overly focused on details. But they were a minority. "There are some musicians, and even some orchestras, for whom hating the conductor is a point of pride," said violist Sam Bergman. "That's not the case here. Moreover, concerts that five or six years ago we might have thought were the pinnacle of what we could do, we now consider average. And while that may not all be due to Osmo, it would be foolish to say that he hasn't contributed to it." Principal Harp Kathy Kienzle recalled Charles Dutoit's return visit to the orchestra podium after an absence of nearly two decades. "He stopped during a rehearsal and said, 'Wow! This orchestra has really changed.'" "It's definitely a happier organization than the one I joined," said trumpeter Charles Lazarus, a member of the orchestra since 2000.

Vänskä seemed more and more at home in Minneapolis. Though he and Pirkko hadn't let go of their house of more than thirty years in Riihimäki, they spent over half the year in Minneapolis, and both had became members of Central Lutheran Church near Orchestra Hall. Neighbors near their home had become accustomed to seeing Vänskä jogging around the neighborhood and, during the warmer months, dodging traffic on his motorcycle. And, in keeping with the notion that Finns get acquainted with others gradually rather than quickly, Vänskä, in time, began to reveal facets of himself that would have been hard to anticipate. He took up the clarinet again, playing publicly, and he began to compose music again. He conducted community orchestras and educational programs for students and led Minnesota Orchestra tours to small towns. He played jazz in a downtown nightclub. He conducted the orchestra in pop music—two concerts of ABBA songs—wearing a 1970s-style ensemble of which Tony

Orlando would have approved. There appeared to be some evidence, in other words, for a statement that Osmo made in a newspaper interview shortly after he arrived: "I'm wilder than people think."

Vänskä's wit came as a surprise, too. Perhaps the stereotype of the dour Finn needs to be retired. Said Kienzle, "A rehearsal doesn't go by that Osmo doesn't say something really funny. A lot of the time it's just putting us at ease. Other times it shows his ability to criticize without making it seem personal. Like he'll be working the first violins over and over on a passage, and he'll say, 'You know, I'm really stubborn and I'm sorry, but I have all the time in the world. If we have to do this forty-five times, so be it. But if you want, we could just do it once.' Or he'll say to a section, 'The person who thinks the rest of the section is late, please play later.'"

In the same vein, the musicians over the years have seen all or most of the conductor's vast collection of t-shirts, one of which carries the banner, "I play in a promising local band." Audiences, too, have experienced Vänskä's humor. There had been word on his arrival that he didn't like to speak to audiences, at least not in English. True or not, he has spoken during the concerts more often as time has gone on and with no apparent difficulty. One evening at Orchestra Hall, he was about to conduct "The Confession of Isobel Gowdie" by James MacMillan, a Scottish composer whom he has championed. Holding a microphone, he told the audience that he had conducted the piece more than once in Europe, and that on one of those occasions a man in the audience who hated the music wanted desperately to boo but couldn't tell when the piece was over because near the end it kept getting softer. Every time he booed, people around him shushed him. Vänskä concluded the story, saying to the audience, "So at the end of the piece, you will see that I will put my arms all the way down, and then you will know it is time to boo."

Vänskä picked up his clarinet again in the summer of 2005. He had been a big admirer of Sommerfest, the four-week summer festival that the orchestra had been putting on at Orchestra Hall since 1980 when Leonard Slatkin, the orchestra's former principal guest conductor, founded the festival and went on to serve as artistic director for its first decade. Sommerfest had had its ups and downs, along with at least two name changes, but by 2005, with the genial conductor-pianist Andrew Litton holding forth as artistic director, the festival was clearly on the upswing and attracting ever-larger audiences. The loose, informal spirit of the original Sommerfest had been recreated to a large extent, and that appealed to Vänskä, who mentioned privately that he wouldn't mind playing in one of the festival's chamber music concerts. Tony Woodcock, then orchestra president, encouraged him, and so the idea became reality: a performance of the Beethoven Clarinet Trio by Vänskä, along with Litton as pianist and Sachiya Isomura, a cellist from the orchestra. Speaking after a rehearsal, Litton said he was impressed. "Osmo plays like he never stopped playing. I wouldn't have a clue that it's been twenty-three years."

"I'm wilder than people think."

(Except for a few chamber music performances, Vänskä had stopped playing publicly in 1982, when he left his position at the Helsinki Philharmonic Orchestra.) More than a few musicians from the orchestra showed up the night of the concert and heard a thoroughly engaging performance. There was an easy give-and-take among the three players and a consistent acknowledgment of the work's classical style in the trim sonorities and buoyant rhythms. Displaying rich tone and fluent phrasing, Vänskä seemed completely at home in this music—and at home onstage as a player rather than a conductor.

In the summer of 2005, Osmo played the clarinet in a Sommerfest concert.

Vänskä continued playing chamber music from time to time both at Orchestra Hall and at the MacPhail Center for Music. In 2007, he took another surprising turn, collaborating with trumpeter Charles Lazarus on a Latin jazz evening as part of Sommerfest. Vänskä conducted, and Lazarus served as host and trumpet soloist in a program, "Night in the Tropics," that included several of his own compositions. That same week the two appeared together at the Dakota, a jazz club in downtown Minneapolis. Vänskä played clarinet in a number that Lazarus had written for him, a lively klezmer-style tune that the two of them with Lazarus's band subsequently recorded on a CD, *Zabava*, released in late 2008.

A year earlier, in October 2006, Vänskä made his Minnesota debut as a composer, leading the orchestra in "Here! . . . Beyond?" a work he had written on the occasion of his fiftieth birthday and premiered with the Lahti Symphony Orchestra during the 2002-2003 season. The piece, which runs just ten minutes, uses a simple, standard form—two fast sections separated by a slow, lyrical segment. The music is smartly orchestrated and clearly articulated, and the central adagio includes a section of impressively passionate writing for strings that soon blazes up to a grand climax for brass. The piece ends in a subdued manner, as if the question of what lies "beyond" has yet to be answered. This respectable debut in composition was followed eighteen months later by "The Bridge," a work commissioned by the Metropolitan Symphony, one of the area's most accomplished community orchestras. Equally brief but more complex and darker in tone, the work was intended as a eulogy for those who lost their lives in the collapse of the Interstate 35W bridge in Minneapolis in August 2007. The music, with its big, violent opening exclamations followed by quick nervous passages from the oboes and clarinets, suggests eruption and connections torn apart. A passage for folk fiddle and then a wistful, lyrical section with a solo flute taking the lead, hint at recovery and re-connection.

Demand for Vänskä as a guest conductor both in Europe and the United States increased during these years, as did the items on his trophy shelf. Musical America named him Conductor of the Year for 2005, and three years later the University of Minnesota presented him with a doctorate of humane letters, a companion to the honorary doctorate he had already received from the University of Glasgow for his work with the BBC Scottish Symphony Orchestra. He also became a regular guest each summer at the Mostly Mozart Festival in New York City. And occasionally he turned down an invitation, as happened with the Los Angeles Philharmonic over the issue of programming. Vänskä asked to do a piece by Aho, a Finnish composer he has championed. The management in Los Angeles said it wanted a more traditional program. Finally, as Vänskä tells the story, since there was no agreement, "I said, 'I don't want to come.' And I cancelled." He admits that it's strange that he has not conducted the Los Angeles Philharmonic, where his old classmate, Esa-Pekka

Salonen, was music director. "I can re-visit Cleveland and Philadelphia," Vänskä said. "I have been almost everywhere, but not Los Angeles. But I have enough things to do. I'm not hungry because I don't get my food from Los Angeles."

The hunt for conspicuous failures during Vänskä's first half-decade with the orchestra doesn't turn up much. True, in the summer of 2003, certain board members argued rather loudly over the choice of orchestra president, and a prominent board member resigned, charging that Vänskä's preference for president was being given more weight than that of members of the board's executive committee. Since this occurred at a time when the orchestra was about to declare a deficit of $2.5 million, the conflict among board members was seen as another potential loss of revenue for the orchestra. In the end, the conflicts were resolved. Tony Woodcock, an Englishman who had managed several orchestras in Great Britain and the United States, became president and immediately formulated a three-year plan to bring the orchestra into the black, an effort that was ultimately successful.

It could be argued, too, that Vänskä's plan to incorporate a team spirit among musicians, staff, management, and even the board hasn't been realized, at least not to the extent that Vänskä and his manager, Tuomas Kinberg, were able to accomplish in Lahti. Sam Bergman recalled the Family Days that Vänskä and Woodcock staged for musicians and board members, a Minnesota version of the Garage Days in Lahti. "The first one was big, the second one not so big, then it stopped," Bergman said. "And we've had occasional orchestra meetings with Osmo, but those haven't been so frequent the past couple of years. I think he felt that for the first couple of years it was important to meet with the whole orchestra and just let us shoot our mouths off. He doesn't see that falling off as necessarily a failure. The regular meetings he sees as more of a European thing. Plus, Lahti has fewer musicians, which makes that sort of thing easier. Getting 100 people in

a room can be productive—or unproductive. But his door is always open. Chiefly, his communication with the musicians is done during rehearsal, and he does have his own way of doing things. He's perfectly willing to hear from you if you want something else, but he's not going to re-make the way he does things to suit you. It's like parenting. Conductors who try to be the orchestra's best friend are like parents who try to be their kid's best friend. The kid might like that, but you're going to run into some problems down the road with that attitude. That is, you have to be an authority figure while being receptive to what's coming from the musicians."

Osmo and concertmaster Jorja Fleezanis confer during rehearsal.

The orchestra's concertmaster, Jorja Fleezanis, agreed that Vänskä is always open to discussion about musical matters, including disagreement, and he might even change his mind. "He never moves right away," she said. "He has to think about it. And, actually, that's good. That creates a better sort of dialogue for the players because they feel they can go to him, sound themselves out, and though you may not get any immediate gratification, that's fine because having time

It's not all "verk" in rehearsal or even in performance. Michael Sutton, a violinist who joined the orchestra in 1997, recalled a mishap of his own during a Thursday morning Coffee Concert. The orchestra was performing Beethoven's Symphony No. 2. "I turned the page," said Sutton. "On the left page is the minuet and trio (the third movement) and on the right is the fourth movement. Everybody started playing the minuet, except me. Instead, I tore into the finale, then muttered this expletive. All around me I could see people shaking violently to keep from laughing. Osmo got beet red. All he could see were people with shoulders shaking, trying to get through this minuet.

The following night, after the second movement, he took off his glasses, as he usually does, and wiped them off. Then he raised his left hand, counted to three, turned to me and said, 'Third movement.' And even though the concert was a broadcast, everybody laughed."

to reflect is the only way he'll do it convincingly. I mean, everything we've done with Osmo has been with the intention that this is a world-class orchestra and that he's going to use his time here with the intention of setting the bar as high as he can, and I think the players like that. The first tour helped solidify his confidence in us, and that confidence was sorely needed, given the fact that we had just had a total—I don't know what to call it—jellyfish year, the year between music directors. So suddenly to have someone come in with the antidote, an antidote that meant we were going to go out on all those famous stages in Europe, that was setting the bar so high that all we could do was work our pants off week after week, working with someone who really believes in you and is going to cut so deep into the artistic possibilities."

Even so, she admits that some of Vänskä's rehearsal techniques are unorthodox, like having the orchestra repeat short phrases over and over. Doesn't that drive musicians crazy? "Not me," she said, "because, honestly, I feel it gets great results. I know, it can be maddening, and around

the third year of doing it, I thought, 'Oh, come on. We can do this differently.' On the other hand, maybe we can't. When you think of getting thirty or forty string players to play a difficult passage, repetition is the way we learn things, like it or not. You can say, 'We've played it once. Let's play it one more time.' It gets a little better. But the likelihood that you've got everybody there at the same place is a crapshoot. Yes, it's also a crapshoot when you do it 800 times. But it decreases the crapshoot percentage a lot. And, in a way, it's a sobering up that has to happen. Most of the problems of ensemble playing are due to lapses in concentration. In a good orchestra like this, everybody can play whatever they're asked to play. It's just that they're not always concentrating at a given moment at the same intense rate. Osmo has really changed that in this orchestra."

Violist Eiji Ikeda, who joined the orchestra in 1979 after playing in the Indianapolis Symphony, said Vänskä is the best music director he has ever worked with. "Osmo respects us," he said, "and he goes after details, like ensemble and intonation, that we needed work on very badly. This was always a good orchestra, but all the music directors we had—Neville, Skrovy, Edo and Eiji—didn't touch the basic, which is ensemble and intonation. They didn't have time. They wanted to work on other things—dynamics or tempo. I'm so happy that we finally got a conductor to care about those things. Osmo's a great orchestra builder. I would give him an A-plus."

Seated in his office one afternoon, Vänskä looked back on his first five years with the orchestra and on life in his adopted city. One wondered in what shape the orchestra was when he took over in 2003. The word "chaos" was heard in various quarters. "To call it chaos is too much," Vänskä said. "I would say there were strong individual opinions about how to play a piece, and often those ideas didn't match one another. There was good playing, but it didn't sound together. That is a typical thing in many orchestras. People's personalities are big, and they believe, 'That's the way I learned it, and that's the way I'm always going to play it.' It wasn't a question of worse or better. But when the orchestra is playing together, the truth is they don't have to lose their individual personalities. We still have some acoustical problems onstage. People have trouble hearing each other. But, as an ensemble, we are playing very well right now. And, dynamically, it's totally different. They have always been able to deliver a forceful sound, but now they can also play much softer, and that gives more color to the whole palette.

"I'd have to say these first five years have been like a 'dog house.' That's what hockey coaches say. It's been a hard time for the players: discipline, discipline, discipline. And so I think that the chance for me right now is that I try to create some kind of freedom based on this discipline. The work that we have done is there, and now we can start to create more and more music.

"It is possible to be too controlling. I have been thinking about this," he said. "My way as a conductor is that I immediately lose my concentration on the music when the ensemble is struggling. My only way to enjoy music is when we are all playing together. Everything comes from that. So right now I see that we have built up this marvelous way of playing together. It's like we are playing chamber music. So what I'm trying to do now is to open my mind and to come out more from this control way of thinking. The control in the rehearsals, we still need to do that. But I think that's the next step for us right now."

He himself has changed during these years. "I hope that I am not the same as when I started. I hope that I have learned things, and it's always when you are working with a really good orchestra that you hear new things, and that gives you good ideas. When everything is in the right place, that's an inspiration for the conductor. When it's one team thinking and breathing in the same way, that's an important school for me, and I hope that I am learning something every day from that."

"The Minnesota Orchestra is a very quick orchestra. They read notes very well and everything is there quite soon."

"In his Minnesota troops, Osmo Vänskä has a real band on his hands, an orchestra with—almost despite the phenomenal balance, clarity, and articulation of the string section—a lean, wiry, fibrous, and muscular quality. . . . Frankly, I could have listened to this lot all night."

Michael Tumelty, *Glasgow Herald*

Helping Young Composers

Orchestra Hall, October, 2007. Osmo Vänskä sits at his desk in his studio, looking intently at the orchestral score in front of him. Across from him is Jacob Cooper, a 29-year-old composer from Connecticut, whose new composition, "Odradek," Vänskä had rehearsed with the Minnesota Orchestra the day before. He would conduct it at a concert

Osmo confers with two young composers.

the following evening. The goal of this meeting is to solve any performance problems that have arisen and to give Cooper, at that time enrolled in the master of musical arts program at the Yale School of Music, the opportunity to make last-minute changes. As Vänskä turns the pages of the score, Cooper asks for several small adjustments. "Really, are you sure about that?" Vänskä says. Over the course of the afternoon, Vänskä meets with six other young composers whose works are being readied for performance. It's obvious that Vänskä has studied these scores carefully. Some of his advice is technical. To Stephen Wilcox, a doctoral candidate in composition at the University of Pennsylvania, he suggests cutting out one of the two trumpets assigned to play a certain passage in a piece titled "Cho-Han." "You don't need two trumpets there," he says. "It's a rule of physics. If two players are playing the same notes, it isn't louder than if only one plays them. With two or three, it's broader, not louder." Other bits of advice are more general. To Cooper he says, "When you are writing, I encourage you to be yourself and not to think too much about others."

Such patient advice from a conductor along with a performance by a major orchestra is a rare experience in the life of a young composer. To hear composers talk about their lives, specifically those who attend this annual Composer Institute in Minneapolis, is to hear a tale of loneliness, frequent rejection, but ever-hopeful persistence against all odds. It's a Catch-22: If you want to write for a symphony orchestra, you need an orchestra to practice on, preferably a good one, and how do you get that chance if nobody knows who you are? But how is anybody going to know you if you don't get that chance?

"This is an odd time for composers right now," said Gregg Wramage, a thirty-nine year old from New Jersey, who attended the Composer Institute in 2006. "Not many of us are getting signed by publishers and being promoted, as was happening in the 1980s and 1990s. These days it's everybody for himself. Everybody's a self-employed individual composer, which means we need to learn the right way to do things and how to be a professional."

Sponsored by the Minnesota Orchestra, the American Composers Forum, and the American Music Center, the week-long Composer Institute is all about teaching composers how to be professional, which means filling them in on things they didn't learn in their conservatories and music departments—subjects like copyright law, grant writing, contracts, career promotion, and, in a quick lesson, how to bow on stage. Mixed with these, in all-day sessions at Orchestra Hall, are seminars more directly related to composition—workshops led by orchestra musicians on how to write clearly for various instruments as well as a rehearsal of a work by each composer. It all leads up to the week's finale, "Future Classics," a public concert with Vänskä, who has put his heart and soul into this institute, leading the orchestra. It's a peak experience that Sean Shepherd, another institute alum, describes as "giving green young composers rides in the back-seat of a Cadillac orchestra with the top down." For many who come here, this will be the first time they have heard a professional orchestra play their music.

The institute was formed during the 1995-1996 season as "Perfect Pitch," an annual series of new-music reading sessions for Minnesota composers. In 1998, when composer Aaron Jay Kernis became the orchestra's new music advisor, he and his co-director Beth Cowart expanded the program to include regional composers. In 2001, the program took on a new title, Composer Institute, and went national, drawing applicants from all over the United States, and adding seminars on business aspects of music, what Kernis calls "the realities of being a composer." Vänskä took an interest in the program and conducted some of the read-throughs in 2005. The following year, he suggested a concert as a finale to the institute, and he has been involved heavily ever since, rehearsing and conducting all the works. "When Osmo added the concert, that kicked the whole thing up a notch," said Cowart.

Kernis, whose String Quartet No. 2 won the Pulitzer Prize in 1998, said nothing of this scope is being done anywhere else. "There are reading programs, but there's not the structured involvement with musicians like this. I had to learn a lot of these things over the years through experience, things we're providing here in a week." Applicants are asked to submit the score of an orchestral work written within the past five years and a recording if available. The initial number of applicants (163 in 2008) is winnowed down by a panel of professional composers, after which Kernis makes the

Each composer had a chance to share his vision for his composition with the orchestra.

final choice. During the institute he works closely with each of the composers, all of whom also receive evaluations from the musicians. Those invited to the institute are given airfare and lodging. Though there is no age restriction, the focus of the program is on composers at the beginning stages of their career.

Many of the composers at the institute found it exhilarating and, at times, unsettling to hear what the products of their imagination actually sound like. "The sounds, of course, are more powerful than when you just look at the score," said Wang Lu, a twenty-six-year-old doctoral candidate at Columbia University in New York City who was born in northern China. She learned of the institute reading a poster at Columbia, and she had heard about it from other composers. "This is a unique program," she said. "It's the only chance we have for an orchestra piece to be heard." The orchestra had just finished rehearsing her piece, "Wailing," which reflects her memory of a scene she witnessed in China at age five: a funeral procession and then a wedding, with much wailing—the winds imitating off-pitch folk instruments—and a wild party after the wedding. "The resonance was very unpredictable," she said. "They're depicting a pageant that gradually gets out of control. But it was too fast. Osmo was following the tempos, which I will have to mark down. They played accurately, but it needed to be more out-of-tune. They aren't trained to play that way."

Not many young composers have an opportunity to hear a professional orchestra play their compositions.

Vänskä meets privately with each of the composers, going carefully over their scores; then, later in the week, he meets with them again. "In the first session, Osmo was all business," said Justin Merritt, a Minnesota composer whose "River of Blood" is based on the 1980 massacre of Salvadoran peasants by right-wing military forces trained by the United States. "It was like: This eighth note, what do you want here? In a very calm way, he wanted to know exactly what I wanted in this piece, and he was going to do it. The second session was about looking at this from the perspective of what we can give to the art. It was a kind of quiet encouragement that I really appreciated."

Why does Vänskä take on a project like this? Wouldn't most music directors palm this off on an assistant? "If there's an assistant conductor, the orchestra often won't take the work seriously," Osmo said. "These pieces are difficult, and to do them well you have to really prepare and concentrate and give it 100 percent of your energy. If not, it will be a bad experience for the composers. What they need is a very good orchestra to play as well as possible, and then they can learn something. I feel also that if we play contemporary music, a work we haven't done before, if we play it well, it makes the orchestra better. And I think this is something for the audience, too, so no one can say, 'They do contemporary music for just two days, and then they go back to their real business.' Well, this is our real business. And I'd have to add that I'm interested in knowing what kind of music the young composers are doing. For me this is like a fresh thing when I'm preparing the scores and studying them. I get a new energy from it. It's a lot of work, yes. But I always say, if you want to make a good dinner, you don't do it in five minutes."

For the seven composers, the daytime sessions were a heady mix of rehearsals and seminars. Evenings were devoted to dinners and, provided the energy held out, recreation. (A group visit to a local bowling alley has become a tradition.)

The speakers that Kernis and Cowart lined up for the seminars offered detailed, practical advice. "Put a spine on your CDs with your name on it, so we can find it on the shelf," said Frances Richard, vice-president and director of concert music for ASCAP, who confided she hates the term "classical music." More advice: "When you do a head shot, do a good one." "Remember, your job is to make a catalogue, and then to look it over. Is there something missing? Do I have a cello concerto? You need a balance of works. If there's a text, don't write the piece until you get permission. Most literary publishers say no automatically. They don't know anything about the musical world, so be persistent. And remember, you want non-exclusive rights or else they won't give it to you."

Evans Mirageas, artistic advisor to the Atlanta Symphony, the Cincinnati Opera, and other organizations, stressed the need for networking and self-promotion. "It's hard for many composers to be aggressive," he said. "Build a following for your music. Get to know various conductors. Work every angle you know. You have a uniqueness that's marketable, and it's up to you to find that market." Maintaining a website, he said, is your primary selling tool. "Think of your website as a department store." And forget about recordings. "There is no EMI anymore, no Decca. It's up to you now." Many suggested niche markets as opportunities, for example, writing for wind ensembles or for children. Jenny Bilfield, drawing on her days as president of Boosey and Hawkes, brought up liturgical music. She recalled writing to a composer, "Your hymn sold a million copies this year." Looking to the future, Mirageas mentioned China. "It's the fastest growing classical music market in the world today. Get your music into China."

Early in the week, two musicians from the orchestra, Concertmaster Jorja Fleezanis and Principal Viola Thomas Turner, spent two hours with the composers, going over their scores and giving them advice on writing for strings and pointing out problems—often in notation. "No matter how great the music is, if it looks ugly on the page, it's not going to get a good performance," said Turner. The goal of the seminar, said Fleezanis, was to establish "certain hot spots" in the scores that might be trouble in rehearsal. Praise was frequent, but many of the comments were in the no-holds-barred vein. Pointing to a passage in Ming-Hsiu Yen's "Yun," Turner said, "We're good players, but this is basically unplayable." Fleezanis agreed. "This ten-tuplet thing is going to be sloppy. I would re-think those bars. We can't possibly be accurate, and that's upsetting for a player." To Antonio

Carlos DeFeo, Turner said, "The slur here looks like one of my eyelash hairs." Fleezanis: "I come to bar 11 and it's Nebraska—too much space. This is a huge eye-training issue." Similar seminars were given on writing for percussion and harp, all held early in the week so that the composers had time to make changes in their scores.

Osmo says, "I'm interested in knowing what kind of music the young composers are doing."

These sessions were all preparation for the main event, the Friday concert. Each composer was interviewed briefly onstage before the piece was played. The mood was up-beat, even irreverent. Asked what advice he would give to a young composer looking to succeed, David Schneider, a twenty-eight-year-old composer from Indiana, said, without skipping a beat, "Choose a different profession." The concert drew

Osmo seems to grasp the composer's obsession and the need for it to be nourished.

about 1,500 people—more each year, and it was largely a young crowd, people who aren't subscribers to the regular season. Listening to the seven pieces, one heard distinct voices from composers of obvious talent and skill. Schneider's "Automation," which depicts a big machine coming to life, then expiring at the end, owes something to the post-minimalism of John Adams, but its intricate, interlocking rhythms and majestic brass writing register their effects in an individual way. Merritt's "River of Blood" opens with waves of violence and closes in a tone of hopeful consolation: soft chimes, ascending intervals, and a solo passage for flute. Ted

Hearne's engrossing "Patriot," with its restless rhythms and distorted military motifs, suggests a sadly ironic meaning to the title, while McManus's "Identity" is a skillfully worked-out mix of opposing elements: triadic tonality and serial atonality. Kernis seemed right on the mark when he said earlier in the week, "A lot of the music this year is dark and dramatic. I think the music very much reflects the world we've been living in."

Whether or not these composers end up with big careers, one thing is clear: Alumni of the institute have prospered, many receiving multiple grants and commissions. "The Composer Institute started a new life for me," said Michael Gatonska, a composer from Connecticut who attended the institute in 2001. "Now I get to hear what I write, and I get to work with some terrific musicians. And it all started in Minneapolis." The Minnesota Orchestra gave the premiere of Gatonska's "In autumn woods a traveler" in the orchestra's main series. Moreover, Gatonska has stayed in touch with many of the composers he met during the institute. "We all support each other," he said. "I wasn't anticipating that." Another alumnus, Dan Visconti, has sustained a relationship with the Minnesota Orchestra. He got a repeat performance of his institute entry, "Black Bend," in the summer of 2007, and in the autumn of 2008 the orchestra premiered a work of his in the Young People's series. In fact, one composer each year is commissioned to write something for that series. "I probably got more out of that institute than from my entire undergraduate experience," Gatonska said. And though Cowart figures that the institute would get more attention if it were located on either coast, the trophy shelf is starting to fill up. Among those trophies: the ASCAP John S. Edwards Award for Strongest Commitment to New Music and from BMI the Outstanding Musical Citizen Award to Cowart and Kernis. Onstage at the 2008 concert, John Nuechterlein, president of the American Composers Forum, presented Vänskä with the forum's annual Champion of New Music Award.

In another reach-out, the concert is available for streaming throughout the world on Minnesota Public Radio the week after the concert.

But there is a bigger award connected to all this. It is considerably less tangible than a plaque, surely more personal and without a doubt more in the vicinity of a life-changing experience. It's the thrill a composer experiences when hearing his or her music played for the first time by a top professional orchestra. That thrill—and all the obsessions and cravings that go along with this strange activity of putting notes on a page—is hard to describe. One of the institute composers, Sean Shepherd, surely got close to it in the blog he wrote right after his first rehearsal during the 2006 institute: "They gave me a beautiful reading. What else could I or any composer ask for in less than an hour? These are moments, and they are so fantastically rare, but they are why we do this thing, why we beat our head against the wall for hours, days, years. I write because, like many composers, I feel that I have to. It just has to be done. And I like to forget how much I crave it. Like any good job, it gets tough at times. Sometimes I have to write, but these experiences remind me how much I want to write."

Vänskä seems to grasp the composer's obsession and the need for it to be nourished. That week he attended a dinner with the composers at a nearby restaurant, after which he made a few remarks. "I told them, 'What if the chefs in the kitchen here are making good food, but no one gets any? It's like the composer who is writing music, but no one is playing it. Maybe they can get a few friends to do their chamber music, but they can't get seventy-five or eighty members of an orchestra to play. That's why we have to take care of them. We have to give them a chance to write and to hear, and they will write even better music the next time.'"

Osmo is also committed to new compositions by established composers. Doc Severinsen and Manny Laureano performed at the world premier of Stephen Paulus' Concerto for Two Trumpets.

"At his best, Osmo Vänskä has the ability
to enter a composer's world with his entire being."

Barbara Jepson, *Wall Street Journal*

Getting It on Disc

The recordings in the Beethoven Symphony set by Osmo Vänskä and the Minnesota Orchestra have received high praise. The *New York Times* reviewer wrote that this "may be the definitive [Beethoven cycle] of our time." The orchestra's recording of Beethoven's Ninth Symphony was nominated for a Grammy for Best Orchestral Performance. (Leonard Slatkin and the Nashville Symphony won the 2008 Grammy for Best Orchestral Performance.) Why a Beethoven set, many asked, when there were, at last count, 125 sets of the symphonies already in the catalogue and this at a time when the entire record industry appeared to be imploding? Vänskä gave several reasons. For one thing, neither he nor the orchestra had ever recorded all nine of the symphonies. And the project offered an opportunity to link the names Vänskä and Minnesota Orchestra in the way that the conductor's name had become closely associated with the Lahti Symphony Orchestra through some seventy-five recordings, several of which had received international awards. Moreover, added Vänskä, teasingly, "Maybe we can bring some fresh ideas to Beethoven."

The idea for the project actually had come not from Vänskä but from Robert von Bahr, president of BIS Records. Perhaps Vänskä, von Bahr had said, could do with Beethoven what he had done with Sibelius. "To hide this kind of music making from the world, just because so many have walked the same road, would be disastrous." Can it pay off? "No idea," he said. "Probably not, since we are investing hugely in this, with state-of-the-art surround-sound on Super Audio CDs and all. Then we have to stand by the sidelines and watch all the computer thieves who will be copying rather than buying the product. It will be hard. Sometimes, however, there are things that have to be done, regardless of money. This is one of them. We will have to sell tens of thousands of each CD to escape with our lives. But if the result is as good as I envision, it is doable. And in the final analysis, this isn't about money, it is about art."

An intense level of concentration is required when an orchestra is making a recording, and maybe doubly so when the material is Beethoven, works that already have been recorded hundreds of times. Mistakes can be edited out. Alternate takes can be patched in. But then there's the matter of the clock. A symphony orchestra is bound by union rules. A three-hour session must include twenty-minute breaks every hour, and

Osmo confers with engineer Ingo Petry and producer Rob Suff.

the costs are daunting: roughly $12,500 an hour just in players' salaries. This makes for an odd equation: The constraints of time and money in the production of a modern orchestral recording call for machine-like efficiency, for an assembly-line sensibility that Henry Ford would have admired, and yet we expect the result—the sounds coming from the shiny five-inch disc to which we listen at home—to be not machine-like at all, but to flow, to be effortless and spontaneous, to be art, to be above all human. And amazingly, it often is so.

The rehearsal room at Orchestra Hall had been set up as the control room/sound booth for the final sessions of Osmo Vänskä's five-year project of recording the Beethoven symphonies for BIS. Producer Rob Suff and engineer Ingo Petry, Vänskä's regular production team, sit at a table on which are two computers, a sound board, and a TV monitor trained on the stage one floor up. The two computers are set up to run simultaneously. "That's for

The rehearsal room at Orchestra Hall is converted into a control room; the clock looms large.

safety," says Petry. The equipment had been shipped from Sweden. At adjacent tables sit the orchestra's operations manager, Beth Kellar-Long, and personnel manager, Julie Haight-Curran, who keeps time for the sessions. A big clock sits prominently on a music stand. Onstage, the orchestra is covered by twenty-six microphones that look like drooping palm trees without leaves. Behind the podium sits a box, a converter that translates sound into digital information to be edited later by Suff.

"This being the fifth series of sessions, the basic set-up for the hall is now very clear," says Petry, who had spent the prior day putting the mikes in place. "The ideal is that it should sound natural. And that means that you don't think you have some kind of artificial orchestra in front of you, but that it's real. But that's not enough. You have to compensate for the non-visual aspect. If the trumpet plays too loudly in a concert, you don't mind so much. But if you hear it on a recording, it sounds worse. That's why we focus so much on details in recording, like getting the rhythm right and the balance. Then we put it all together."

The afternoon session was about to begin, and everyone, understandably, looked tense. No one was talking. And yet there was a feeling of confidence in the room, and not only because these were long-time colleagues.

The art began when Vänskä stepped to the podium. "Are you OK? Fine, thank you," he said to the musicians, all in one breath, then gave a downbeat for the second movement of Beethoven's Symphony No. 7. He stopped right away, asked the woodwinds to tighten up the opening chord, then continued the movement through to the end. Meanwhile, down in the rehearsal room, Suff, wearing earphones, sat with the score in front of him (the more recent Barenreiter edition), continually making notes in pencil. When the music stopped he spoke into his microphone. Unlike in many orchestra recording set-ups, his voice could be heard onstage by both musicians and conductor. "Could we do the ending first, Osmo?" They start at bar 234. Suff: "Could the horns play a bit softer when they play together? At 203: Violins not precisely together." After a few more corrections, Vänskä leads a furious run-through of the finale. When Suff calls for a break, several of the musicians—concertmaster Jorja Fleezanis, violinist Michael Sutton, principal trumpet Manny

Laureano, principal viola Thomas Turner—file quickly into the room and listen to the playback of the finale, during which Vänskä and Suff confer. The break over and everyone back in place, Suff offers comments: "The first four bars aren't clear enough." "Bar 12 isn't together." "Timpani, bar 28 was late." "First four bars weren't explosive enough."

The sessions continue on the second day. Vänskä leads the orchestra through the second movement of Symphony No. 2. After the final chord he says to Suff on the intercom, "They want to know if they were late or early." Suff replies, "Well, in one place they were late, and in another they were early." There's a break and a playback of that same movement. Vänskä enters to listen. His t-shirt is darkened with sweat.

At the final recording session, in the final minutes of a project that has engaged these people for four years, Suff names three passages he would like to correct. "We have only nine minutes to do it," he says. "We're looking for another version of 330 in the finale and of bars 198 through 204 in the second movement and bar 278 in the finale." They run through these quickly and efficiently and then stop. Suff speaks into his microphone. "I'd come out onstage and talk to you, but we have only two minutes. I just want to say that it's been an inspiration and a privilege to work with all of you. The time these four years has gone all too quickly. This is a truly great orchestra and a wonderful achievement." Through the loudspeaker we hear the musicians applauding. In less than a minute Jorja Fleezanis enters, walks right to Suff, and embraces him, then embraces everyone in the room. "I can't say enough about what you've done," she says to Suff, "and I feel very sad that this is over. But we now have this important credential that's out there."

Just outside the rehearsal room, the orchestra's acting associate principal bass, William Schrickel, stands at his seven-foot-tall locker, putting his instrument away. He looks

exhausted. "This is my thirty-first year in the orchestra," he says. "I feel like I've waited my whole career for this to happen. I'm very proud of these recordings. It took Osmo's coming here to get this accomplished."

Vänskä talked about his recording career. Vänskä and the Lahti Symphony Orchestra became known internationally for the vigorous and revealing performances of Sibelius for BIS Records' Sibelius Edition. The Vänskä catalogue of some ninety discs (see page 125) also includes generous samplings of works by contemporary Finnish composers such as Aho, Kokkonen, Klami, and Rautavaara, along with a much-

The control room gets crowded when it's time to evaluate the recorded tracks.

admired set of the Nielsen symphonies with the BBC Scottish Symphony Orchestra. Mainly, though, it was the awards that Vänskä and the Lahti orchestra earned for their initial efforts in the Sibelius repertoire (among them Gramophone's Record of the Year in 1991 for the original version of the

Violin Concerto with Leonidas Kavakos and the Grand Prix du Disque two years later for "The Tempest") that announced to the musical world that here was an orchestra and a conductor capable of putting intriguing performances on disc, and attention needed to be paid.

Osmo explains to the orchestra sections which must be re-recorded.

Without an audience, how do you get the live atmosphere during recording sessions?

Osmo: There's a philosophy behind it. I always think that the conductor should "conduct from the front," which means not only asking people to do things but to show through body language that I am very serious and that's the way I want them to play, too. The most important thing is to keep up the spirit so that we can get good phrasing and a lot of good energy. That's my job. I know that there are many great conductors who do it differently. They are much less physical. But I can't do it that way. If I start to pull back and make small movements, I feel I'm losing the music. I feel like an outsider. I feel like, how can I ask these musicians to give everything they've got if I don't give everything? That's my only way to make music, and that happens in every rehearsal and every concert. And it's even more so in recordings because we don't have an audience. We have to get excited on our own.

Ingo Petry, the recording engineer, says that in Beethoven you try to stay ten percent slower than the infamous metronome markings.

Osmo: There have been many opinions about Beethoven's metronome. Was it working correctly or not, and so on. My idea about the composer is that I have to be as loyal as possible. I try to go to those tempos that are marked and that we believe are from Beethoven himself. But in some instances I believe that it then gets too fast and it doesn't work. So then I have to make some kind of guideline because I don't think it's correct for me if one day I think one thing and something else another day. There must be a connection to Beethoven. It's simple. If I feel that we cannot go for that number, then I count ten percent down. It's funny, and I don't know why, but it's usually in the first and second movements that I have to do that. Then in the finale, we are very much on the metronome mark.

You and Suff obviously trust each other. If you have disagreements, how do you settle them?

Osmo: We never have had big arguments. We have had different opinions, but we have found it easy to come together. There are stories about conductors and producers fighting for control and power, but we haven't had that. I think that, finally, it's the conductor who should make the decisions, but I have been so lucky with Suff because he really understands what I want and how I want to do music. He doesn't try to impose his own views, or it may just be that our tastes are similar. And he has given me some ideas: "Are you sure you want it this way?" And I have learned that when he says something, I have good reason to listen. It has been for us a kind of mutual respect because I know that he is a really good musician.

Did the success of your Sibelius Violin Concerto with Kavakos surprise you?

Osmo: I guess so. We knew that this was something special, but we were surprised when we started getting these huge reviews. But the fact is we worked very hard. On the other hand, if you work and work and work but you don't get any comments from outside Lahti, it's difficult to keep the spirit going on. So when we got those reviews for the concerto and then the Gramophone award, it told us we were doing good things, so let's continue. And that happened every time we got good comments, especially from London or New York.

You have done more than ninety discs for BIS. Is there one you'd like most to re-record?

Osmo: No, when we have done something, it is a documentation of that time and of that person at that time. I'm not the same person, the same conductor, that I was fifteen years ago. I'd feel silly re-doing one of them. Who says it is better now? It's different, but not necessarily better. BIS has said that they might want to have new Sibelius recordings once again with me, and right now I'm thinking, "No way." They would like to have them in this Super Audio sound and do them with the Minnesota Orchestra. My feelings are "No." But, who knows?

What has been your biggest seller?

Osmo: I think it's still the Violin Concerto, the original version. But they have all sold quite well. Even the recordings of Aho and Kokkonen have sold many thousands.

Later that day, producer Rob Suff sat in the Green Room at Orchestra Hall and talked about this project and his long association with Vänskä and the Lahti Symphony Orchestra, beginning in 1992 when the two of them collaborated on the first complete recording of Sibelius's incidental music for "The Tempest." The partnership by 2008 accounted for about forty discs. Suff, a Welshman, is tall and solemn looking but quick to laugh. Trained as an oboist and conductor, he holds a degree in music from King's College, London. He calls it "a twist of fate" that he ended up a record producer. He names

Von Bahr as his teacher in the esoteric art and science of record production. This was his fifth visit to Minneapolis, and there would likely be more visits, given that the orchestra had announced plans to record the Anton Bruckner symphonies. Looking back on the Beethoven project, now almost finished, Suff recalled the first step in the project back in 2004, recording Beethoven's Symphony No. 5. They did it in two three-hour sessions the first day, completing the final take just ten seconds before the scheduled end of the second session, an experience he described as one of the most tense moments he had ever been through in his many years of recording.

How would you characterize the Minnesota Orchestra, both in sound and style?

Suff: I don't think the orchestra here has an easily recognizable sound. It's more the qualities in the playing: the precision of ensemble, the intonation, the phrasing, and the general approach that Osmo takes and that we try to help him reproduce—the clarity of texture and balance. I mean, if you put this recording up against another one, you might after a while say, "OK, that must be Vänskä and Minnesota because the same characteristics reappear." And I must say, most important in this context is the way that this orchestra and Osmo have managed to combine what is still essentially a big-band Beethoven sound with a chamber-music-like quality. What Osmo has done, I think, is to refine it and chisel it and get the transparency but not to emasculate the sound. It's still a full, modern symphony orchestra playing with full tone production, and sometimes that's difficult because, when he asks them to play really softly and with less vibrato, there's the danger that the tone quality suffers.

What do you recall about your first collaboration, "The Tempest"?

Suff: It was clear right away that Osmo and I had established a personal as well as musical rapport, and that was cemented,

"Osmo is the ideal recording conductor. He never gives up. The focus and the physical commitment in his conducting is the same in the last take on the last day as it was starting out."

Rob Suff

I think, when we did the Sibelius project in Lahti. When you work on seven symphonies by the same composer, it's like making a journey together, and we recorded them chronologically, except that we started with the original version of the Fifth Symphony, as kind of a test case. It's been a developing and evolving relationship. And, of course, when you work with a conductor, you have to share his ideals. It's the job of a professional producer to support the artist, and you can support the artist even if you don't believe 100 percent in what he does. But you have to criticize if you don't agree. We've had serious disagreements only once or twice. I emphasize the relationship because in order for this to work, the trust has to be there. When we started Beethoven here in 2004, Osmo and I had already worked together for twelve years. So even though I can't explain why we hear things in a similar way, we both know what each expects of the other. Osmo knows what I'm going to ask for, and I know how far he wants to go. It's nothing telepathic. It's just something that evolves.

Robert von Bahr, the president of BIS, has said that the first Vänskä-Lahti recording, the Crusell clarinet concertos, was a disaster. He said the sessions were "a catastrophe" and that he would never return to Lahti. He did, of course, return two years later.

Osmo: *It's a very good CD. There are no mistakes. Robert's comment is typical of his responses. He dramatizes things. It was a difficult recording session, I agree with him on that. We needed many takes. But, finally, the playing wasn't bad. We needed some extra takes, too, from the soloist, Karl Leister, who was very good, and he was able to play them again. There were places where the soloist played well but the orchestra didn't. I know it was a disappointment for Robert. But it wasn't catastrophic. He believes that we are not allowed to make mistakes. He means well, but it just doesn't work. We have had big fights, but I still love him. He has done great service for contemporary music. And I'm thankful that he gave me a chance to do things with the Lahti Orchestra. I know that without Robert, without BIS, my career wouldn't be what it is now. It has been one of the most important things in my life.*

What is the producer's role?

Suff: As producer, even if I don't do the editing, I choose the takes to be used and make the editing plans. I'm building up the concept as I go along: "OK, this will fit with this." Whereas I see the post-production work as putting together all the best moments, and the only rule is that you don't destroy the line. It should sound as if they'd only played it once. It's a fine line. It's not a matter of willfully manipulating anything. It's just that more possibilities open up. And as long as you're not going against the spirit of the music and the intentions of the performers, then in the end nobody knows. That's the challenge.

Is it usual that the producer's comments during the sessions are audible to the entire orchestra?

Suff: It depends on the conductor and his ego and his preferred way of working. If I say something that's critical of Osmo in front of the whole orchestra, he's man enough to accept it. He's not playing God. He trusts my opinion.

Will Osmo hear the first edit?

Suff: Yes, I'll send him a CD. We've worked so long together, he'll probably hear it just once. He trusts me. I know he listens because some of his comments are very detailed and, for my purposes, that's great. He's not asking for some kind of mystical performance that doesn't exist. He knows what we have done, and he accepts that what I give him is the way it was.

Is the producer often a better judge of the performance than the conductor?

Suff: The producer has to function as the conductor's second pair of ears, and ideally as his alter ego, and on all levels, give him moral support, constructive criticism, all those things. In the end, ninety percent of it is psychology and ten percent is music, though I'd have to say that when you're working with an orchestra on this level, I usually don't have to explain things. I just have to say, "Again, please," because they already know what's wrong.

Osmo is the ideal recording conductor. He never gives up. The focus and the physical commitment in his conducting is the same in the last take on the last day as it was starting out. Partly, it's that he's so fit. He exercises, which means he doesn't get tired at the podium. I mean, you conduct the finale of the Seventh Symphony four times in an hour and, of course, you're exhausted. You can see other great conductors on film, like Karajan, who never made wild gestures. But then look at Osmo conducting the finale of the Seventh. He's working very hard to keep the whole machinery going, and that's a strength. He's trying to make it sound as much as possible like a live experience.

Should records seek to duplicate the concert hall experience or is it a different medium and therefore subject to quite different technical and artistic considerations?

Suff: Ideally, it should be an idealized concert experience. It should be as exciting and engaging as a good live concert but with a perfection that is seldom achieved live. With the surround-sound you can replicate a little more the big hall feeling, the open sound, without having to record it objectively; that is, we're not recording much of the hall in this project. We tried to go for a fairly tight sound, not too much of the hall, and to go for a clarity and punchiness.

Do you think this will be the last commercial set of the Beethoven symphonies?

Suff: No. As long as there are conductors on a career path, there will always come a point where somebody will want to do a Beethoven cycle, if only because the music is so great. And there will always be an audience for it. We can, of course, hark back to earlier days and say, "I love my Furtwängler Ninth from 1951 or my Toscanini from 1926," or whatever, whereas younger people will make the journey in reverse. They grow up in the digital age, and if they buy the actual physical product rather than downloading, they'll use the past ten years as a starting point and then work backwards. So there will always be a new audience there. And a fine orchestra like this, since the time of Dorati, hasn't been in the public perception, at least not in Europe. So to do a project like this is of incalculable importance because, if it's good, people will take notice.

The trust between Osmo and producer Rob Suff is apparent.

"Here is the modern Beethoven recording par excellence."

Andrew Clark, London *Financial Times*

"I think the result is better and better
if we work very closely.
But it is also a challenge, because if our
relationship is very, very close,
then it is also very delicate
and we need to find the right words,
right methods to work so that we
still have respect for each other.
We need to rehearse very carefully,
and at the same time take care that
the music is always there,
that we go beyond playing notes correctly."

Osmo Vänskä

Music with a Finnish Touch

Every Finnish conductor is acquainted
with the music of Jean Sibelius,
whose works are central to Finnish culture.

Finnish Conductors

Two people who are intimately acquainted with the musical scene in Finland have followed Osmo Vänskä's career for nearly two decades. Kai Amberla is director of Finland Festivals, a lobbying organization for the festival business in Finland. From 1995 to 2001 Amberla was director of the Association of Finnish Symphony Orchestras, and previously he served as director of the Finnish Music Information Center. Vesa Sirén is the music critic of the *Helsingin Sanomat*, the daily newspaper in Helsinki. Sirén is a walking encyclopedia of Finnish musical history.

Is there such a thing as a Finnish school of conductors, a style or a technique that they share?

Sirén: If there is a Finnish school, it's a Panula school. The idea is you don't talk much. You want to show as much as you can with your hands. I would say that Osmo talks a little bit more than some other people from the Panula school, and that might even help him because he's very precise in what he wants. You can show nearly everything with your hands, of course, but it's easier if you can add some words. But they don't talk much in rehearsal, which means that you get to play more at rehearsals than, say, with Nicholas Harnoncourt, who explains and explains. But also, because of the video training, they don't have the mannerisms that bother musicians. And the other thing is they all have individual techniques because Jorma Panula didn't push only one technique. You had to find your own way of phrasing. He doesn't say, for example, that you should conduct with a stick or without. He doesn't

use one himself, but most of his students do. And to prevent someone from copying his individual technique, Panula doesn't beat time much. He does phrasing, but not much time beating, though he demanded time beating from his students whenever they needed it. These are the common things. And, of course, that leaves room for great individuality.

How are they different at the podium: Salonen, Saraste and Vänskä?

Amberla: Salonen seeks a more sensual sound, while Osmo's style is more driven, more intense. But the control is very strict in Salonen also, though many people say there is now a California influence on his communication, both as a composer and a conductor, which wasn't the case when he was young. He really wants to have a dialogue with the audience.

Of course, all performers are looking to communicate, but for Osmo the communication is aimed at showing the audience what the composer wanted. He's more strict. He also tends to decline to talk about his interpretations, saying only that he's faithful to the score. That's a nice philosophy, but what do you mean by that? It's always an interpretation, whatever they do. It's not the final truth.

Saraste is a bit closer to Osmo. Saraste is very strict, and he can be nasty, whereas Salonen is a nice guy. Everybody loves him. Vänskä and Salonen aren't close, as far as I know, but I suppose there is a mutual respect, whereas Salonen and Saraste are friends. Salonen is kind of a god here. He does the Helsinki Festival every year, also the Baltic Sea Festival. Both are always sold out.

Sirén: People say it's real easy to play with Osmo conducting. Esa-Pekka [Salonen] also used to be the most crystal clear time beater, and then he found out that something was lacking. Nowadays, he does much more phrasing and much less time beating than he used to do. He tries to do slow movements without a stick, which didn't work at first, for me at least, but now it works beautifully. They change over the years. Esa-Pekka has changed a lot. Jukka-Pekka [Saraste] changed extremely. He had one technique, then he thought, "I should stop this time-beating business and do like Furtwängler did," which means the broad line and not doing much, leaving more for the principals to do. This didn't work with the Finnish Radio Symphony very well because he didn't have the principals. Osmo, I think, hasn't changed so much. His technique is more or less the same, except that he is more relaxed and more confident.

Certainly Osmo is in the top three of Finnish orchestra builders. Robert Kajanus, who created his own school, is another, and a third is Paavo Berglund, who worked all through the 1960s with the Finnish Radio Symphony. With Osmo it goes back to religion. The first phase of any interview with Osmo, if you ask about composers and conducting, he always says, "I stick to the score," which is very much the same as a religious person does with the Bible: When in doubt, research, think about it, and you will find the way. That's his attitude toward the score. The truth is there. So if you just concentrate and think and try to do what it says, you will be OK. In a way, it might be some kind of salvation. If you work hard, it will be OK. Whether it's Aho or Beethoven or Sibelius, he searches for something unifying, maybe something holy—an experience of holiness in music, which is not necessarily what Esa-Pekka searches for. Esa-Pekka started as a very strict modernist conductor, stern-faced. Then he went into his hedonistic phase, where what he wanted to do was have a party together with the music and the audience. Whereas now I think he is searching for a more refined, delicate sound.

Are you surprised at Vänskä's success in America?

Sirén: Osmo Vänskä was always good, but he didn't have the kind of start that Esa-Pekka had or even that Jukka-Pekka had when he was nominated to the Toronto Symphony. When Jukka-Pekka started there in 1997, that was big news in Finland. And, of course, he started getting many American orchestras then, too. So what you had was Esa-Pekka, world-famous superstar. You had Jukka-Pekka, rising star in Toronto and Helsinki. And then there was their classmate Osmo, who was stuck in Lahti. But because of the Sibelius recordings on BIS, which won a lot of awards, he wasn't stuck in Lahti anymore. Lahti was becoming a significant place getting international attention. This was in 1996. So after a start that wasn't so fast and without many breaks, he got one lucky break after another: the Sibelius Violin Concerto—a good recording; the Fifth Symphony—an excellent recording; and then "The Wood Nymph."

And then that year he was also with the Iceland Symphony Orchestra, which nobody thought anything about. But they toured, visiting places like Sarasota and Orlando—not very important—but they did do one concert at Carnegie Hall. And, again, Osmo was lucky. *The New York Times* sent Alex Ross to review it. The result: a rave. I asked Osmo what happened. I knew he hadn't said so many good things about the Iceland Symphony in those years. He said it was an enormous challenge, "We played Sibelius in eight concerts, so that the last one at Carnegie Hall was pretty good. Everyone was very enthusiastic and wanted to show off." I asked him whether the rave review from *The New York Times* would change his life. He said, "I don't know. People in the U.S. say my life will not be the same, which is absurd. Anyway, you cannot do music worrying about what other people will think. But if the reviews are good, we will make use of that." That same year, he was appointed chief conductor of the BBC Scottish Symphony, and he came to be the darling of the London press, because he's a great orchestra builder.

So, given this evolution, I'm not surprised that Osmo has done well in the U.S. Partly, it was that the timing was right. A recording of the Beethoven symphonies would have been viewed as a ridiculous idea just five years earlier. Everyone then was fed up with mediocre Beethoven cycles by superstar conductors. But the precision and sound of these recordings were good. Part of the attraction of the Minnesota set was that it was one of the first in the new SACD surround-sound format. And, so far, the critics love SACD.

What are Osmo's strengths as a conductor?

Amberla: He doesn't fake it. He takes things seriously, even doing ABBA. He rehearses all the time. He's interested in music, not in a career. And he wants to get the orchestras he works with to play as well as possible. He saw the potential in Lahti, for example, which when he arrived was a pitiful orchestra. And their hall was bad, too. I think it's that he's willing to put a lot of time and energy into things other people wouldn't do. Esa-Pekka, for instance, would never have gone to Lahti.

"Whether it's Aho or Beethoven or Sibelius, he [Osmo] searches for something unifying, maybe something holy— an experience of holiness in music."

Vesa Sirén

Finnish Composers

Jean Sibelius

Two names have become intertwined in recent years—Vänskä and Sibelius—chiefly through the superlative recordings of the Sibelius orchestral works that Osmo recorded with the Lahti Symphony Orchestra for BIS. Every Finnish conductor, of course, has some acquaintance with the music of Sibelius, whose works are central to Finnish culture, though it's equally true that some of those conductors, as they developed international careers, resisted being typecast as Sibelius specialists. "Just at the moment, I don't really see why I of all people should be recording Sibelius symphonies," said Esa-Pekka Salonen in an interview in *The Finnish Music Quarterly.*

Vänskä's case was different. He often conducted the Sibelius symphonies and tone poems early in his career, he once said, because not many conductors were doing that repertoire. The rage at that time was for Mahler. When BIS selected Vänskä and Lahti as the official conductor and orchestra for the Sibelius Edition and these recordings began to win international awards, the connection was established between the three—conductor, composer, and orchestra. These are striking performances—taut and acerbic, Sibelius without cushions, bleak at times, modernist rather than romanticized. If this is Sibelius for the twenty-first century, Osmo goes back to the original scores, for that was—and continues to be—his obsession: nothing but what the composer intended.

Jean Sibelius

You once said that when Sibelius died in 1957, your mother cried. All Finns cried. Does Sibelius still have this importance, or is it only older Finns who feel this?

Osmo: Even today there is no Finn who doesn't know Sibelius. I can give you my guarantee about that. It's a small country, and he's still important. Even teenagers know Sibelius and what he did. He's one of the most important twentieth-century composers, and I think he will become even more important. He was quite modern, but they didn't understand that in earlier times. Listen to the Seventh Symphony. At the same time, he had a connection to the tradition too. Germans called him provincial. Those writers thought that all music should sound like German music. Actually, Sibelius used the same methods as Schubert and Mozart and Beethoven, who all used German folk music. Sibelius did the same, using Nordic folk tunes, though he always denied using them.

You have called the Sibelius symphonies "deep waters," and you said, "There is a godly presence in this music." Do you bring your own religion into your reading of this music, or do you think a religious spirit exists in the works themselves?

Osmo: If a man is a doctor, is he a doctor only when he is doing his job or is he always a doctor? Is someone a Christian only when he is going to church or also when he leaves the church? This is a big theological question.

For me, music is about our life, about human life. If Shostakovich felt that the Communist system was the biggest threat to his life or to the life of others, if he felt that this one individual was going to be killed or ruined, and the system was putting pressure on him, you can still hear in his music a kind of hope. I'm not so keen on giving a name to that hope. Is it coming from the God of the Christians? Is it coming from the God of the Jews? Or is it coming from the Asian God? Those kinds of things are less and less important for me right now. Do you name your God this way or that way, and if you don't say it this way, then you are terrible? Human beings make so many rules about God that they end up believing that they are bigger than God. People like to put everything into different boxes, and if you do what that box says, it's terrible. Ideas like that come from human beings, not from God. The big questions of religion are so huge that no one can understand them. That's why I think that music is a good example for us. You can hear in some music that someone is really sad. Or you listen to Shostakovich or Beethoven or to Sibelius—the Fifth or Sixth or Seventh Symphonies—and the music tells you that there is some kind of hope for human beings. And if someone wants to describe these as religious connections, do so. But we cannot say for certain whether Beethoven's hope comes from what a priest says is the right kind of God and therefore that's what Beethoven thought or whether the God of Sibelius is the same or different. Who

cares? What we need is some consolation, the feeling that things are fine. This is life. And that's what impresses me when we are playing. Sometimes the feeling is that there is no hope. Other times there is a bigger hope than ever.

Colin Davis thinks of the ending of the Sibelius Symphony No. 4 as "dark," that it suggests that "death is no consolation," whereas you see the same music as more hopeful.

Osmo: Yes, for me that ending offers some kind of light, the idea that, even though I don't understand why things are so complicated, the light is still there. It's not fanfares and flags, but it's not only death. There's also some kind of hope, and it's not like I'm announcing it. It's simply saying that somewhere in my life there is hope, even when things are going the wrong way.

Your recording of Sibelius's First Symphony has some of the same quality as Kajanus' recording. Were you influenced by the Kajanus discs?

Osmo: The truth is I didn't hear the Kajanus recording until after I had done my own. As for tempos and things in that symphony, it's simple. It's allegro for the first movement, and Sibelius gives the metronome timing. So I do it fast, but that's following Sibelius, not Kajanus. And if you do it fast like that, it sounds wild. Now a lot of people today say it's too fast. Hey, it's a young man's music. He was a young composer, around thirty. I think the problem is many people think of Sibelius as some kind of old maestro. No, he was young, and he wanted to prove that he was a good composer, which people didn't believe at that time. He was coming from a very small country, and he wanted to be discovered, and so there is this kind of drive in the music.

Sibelius's chief biographer, Tawastjerna, quotes Sibelius on Tchaikovsky: "There is much in the man that I recognize in myself." Some hear a Russian influence in the first two symphonies. Do you?

Osmo: I agree somewhat, but if someone is saying there is this kind of sentimental sweetness, no. That is not being loyal to Sibelius who was a young composer at the time of the First Symphony. For me, Sibelius's music is not sentimental, especially not in the first two symphonies. Usually, the first movement of the First Symphony isn't taken fast enough, which makes it sound like Tchaikovsky's ballet music. If you take it fast, there is no sentimentality. It's much wilder and stronger if you keep it going, as Sibelius wanted, and I think that if you do it that way, people don't connect the music so much with Russia.

There is an evolution in the performances of Sibelius' music through the twentieth century. Kajanus in the 1930s performed Sibelius with a real push, fast and exciting. With Leonard Bernstein and Herbert von Karajan and Colin Davis in the 1960s and 1970s, this music gets slower and smoother. Your performances are more detailed, with more contrast and steadier tempos.

Osmo: Yes, it's written that way: one steady tempo. A typical example is the Fourth Symphony, the slow movement. The others don't have the discipline to keep it slow. It's the same in Dvořák: They start the allegro after the introduction very fast, which means they have to slow down for the second subject.

My solution is to take the first allegro slightly slower, so that I will be able to continue in the same tempo for the second subject. I don't want to go up and down in tempo. The backbone of the music must be strong enough to keep it going.

Did your understanding of Sibelius develop gradually?

Osmo: It was a question I thought about for a long time: how to do it. First, I played eleven years in an orchestra and played a lot of those pieces many times, and I learned a certain way of doing them. And when I was studying conducting, I thought, "Maybe I should do it the same way." But I wasn't convinced. Then something happened, something that was a turning point in my life as a conductor, not only for Sibelius but for other composers, too. But it happened with a Sibelius symphony, the original version of the Fifth Symphony. In the end, in both versions, the score says pochissimo largamente [a little bit slower]. But there's a difference in the original version. There's a place where the woodwinds are playing. [He sings the rhythm.] If you do it as if it were the final version, it's more like molto largamente [much slower], and it's actually impossible to do. I still remember as I was studying the original version, I thought, "Why do we do the same thing in the final version so much slower?" I looked at the score, and for the first time I recognized pochissimo largamente, that is, a small slowing down. But tradition was doing moltissimo. I felt like I was waking up. If the composer wants pochissimo, why do we do molto? I started to read scores in a new way. What if the composer really meant what he wrote? I had to change my thoughts. The score is the only way the composer can communicate to the performer. So who am I to change something in the score? When I hear a Sibelius performance that I think is interpreted wrong, I don't want to listen. Of course, I have to allow my colleagues to do it their way, but I cannot listen. If it's radio or CD, I turn it off. It's much better to listen to those pieces that I don't know.

Paavo Berglund says he had to correct many things in the parts for the symphonies, and he even changed some orchestration. When you studied the manuscripts, did you make changes?

Osmo: I know that he has done it. I don't, except for very small changes, like taking the basses an octave lower. But I also know that Paavo is very loyal to the composer. If he changed something, it was most likely that he thought this would bring the performance closer to the original score. That's what I'm guessing.

Sibelius said that Symphonies No. 3 and No. 4 don't need a big orchestra. Do you think all the symphonies are more effective with a smaller orchestra or just some of them?

Osmo: Almost all of them were written for the Helsinki Philharmonic. At that time they had twelve first violins and then maybe ten, eight, seven, and five [second violins, violas, cellos and basses], something like that—exactly the Lahti size. Whereas, today you have sixteen, fourteen, and so on. This is the modern system. What Sibelius knew was the smaller orchestra, like Lahti. I never had balance problems with Lahti in the Sibelius symphonies, even when we were on tour—and we played in all kinds of halls. The Lahti brass players always had great discipline. They never over-powered the other instruments. What probably prompted Paavo Berglund was that when you have a smaller orchestra with high quality players, there is a greater transparency and tighter rhythms. That's what I try to do with the Minnesota Orchestra, that we always play so well and so together that there is not this kind of tiny echo when someone is always behind the others. That's the key thing. But I'm sure that Paavo got very satisfactory performances from the Chamber Orchestra of Europe because, for one thing, they like him. And also with a smaller orchestra, the woodwinds don't have to play so loud. They can keep a beauty to their sound. Bigger is not always better.

Have you ever thought of using a smaller version of the Minnesota Orchestra for Sibelius?

Osmo: No, because if the discipline is there, a big orchestra can play even softer than a smaller orchestra. It's a question of whether they are doing the same piece. If they're doing the same piece, the big string section is a great toy. It can play like a chamber orchestra, but it also has huge power if needed, and that's what I love.

Is there any similarity in the way Finnish conductors approach Sibelius?

Osmo: It's very individual. You might have as many interpretations as you do conductors. But one thing they share: The Finns always know the tradition. At the least they know how the music used to be played. So if I depart from the tradition, it's not because I don't know the tradition.

Sibelius destroyed his manuscripts late in life; among those manuscripts presumably was his Symphony No. 8. Why do you think he did it?

Osmo: There are many theories. I believe that he had become so self-critical and that he was scared that he couldn't compose on the same level as the Seventh Symphony and "Tapiola." I don't know. He was under such pressure from so many people and all the newspapers around the world saying, "Where is the Eighth Symphony?" And also, we know he enjoyed alcohol. There must have been some kind of depression, and when you are drunk you might feel much more dramatic. I suspect he wasn't very cool when he made that decision. Who knows?

Jean Sibelius

If you could sit with him and talk, what would your first question be?

Osmo: I would say, "Thank you for all the great music you have written." I don't think I would ask him questions about his music because he wrote it so well. The music is there. You just take it and play it. I also think that he was OK with different kinds of interpretations of his music. The music was the most important thing to him, not how it was played. He said in the Jalas book, talking about a performance of the Fourth Symphony by Sir Thomas Beecham, that Beecham didn't slow down at the end. He said, "It works well that way." Then he added, "But if the conductor is not very skillful, it's better not to try this." That's a message. He didn't write anything in the score about slowing down, but his comment suggests that if you're not sure of what you're doing, maybe it's natural to slow down. So the question is: Which way did you want it? I'm tempted to say: If the conductor is skillful, he wanted it played as written.

You speak so often in admiration of composers like Sibelius who write music about life and humanity and about sadness and joy. How do you respond to music that is more abstract? You aren't a big enthusiast of the Second Viennese School?

Osmo: Correct. But I have done some things: Schoenberg, Webern, and Berg. I enjoyed those. Let's take the Passacaglia by Webern. Is there a piece that is more expressive and giving? And it isn't so serial in technique as what he wrote later. But as far as the whole Second Viennese School, I wouldn't say I wouldn't touch it, but it's not my first choice. It's music that doesn't give you back anything unless it's very well done. There are a few pieces, like Schoenberg's Chamber Symphony, that I am ready to do. But when I'm invited to conduct an orchestra, they don't ask me to do these things, and I don't want to push very hard because there are so many other composers to do. So they might be on my list, but way down.

Kalevi Aho

Kalevi Aho is perhaps the most prominent Finnish composer of his generation, a prolific creator of chamber music, vocal works, and large-scale orchestral pieces that contain the "multitudes" (the polyglot idioms and ironies) associated with the music of Mahler and Shostakovich. The author of more than 400 articles on music and other cultural subjects, Aho has enjoyed a long and fruitful relationship with Vänskä and the Lahti Symphony Orchestra. As one of their first discs for the BIS label in 1989, they recorded Aho's Symphony No.1 and his Violin Concerto. He became composer-in-residence with the Lahti orchestra in 1992. Since then Vänskä and the orchestra have given the premiere of several of his concertos and five of his symphonies, including Symphony No. 11 for Percussion Sextet and Orchestra, which was premiered at the concert that opened Sibelius Hall in 2000. Aho described that event as "one of the greatest triumphs of my career as a symphonist." Vänskä has programmed both Symphonies No. 7 and No. 9 during his years with the Minnesota Orchestra.

Aho said he has felt quite at home in the new Lahti hall and with the orchestra. He said he probably wouldn't have composed as much orchestral music as he has—thirteen symphonies at last count—were it not for his close tie to the Lahti orchestra, a connection that gave him not only assurance that his works would be performed, but also that they would find an audience. "I know now the sound of this orchestra and also the personality of the principals who will be playing the solo parts," Aho said. "I've learned so much from this relationship. For example, this orchestra has such a good tuba player, for whom I have written several solos. Before then I never had written tuba solos. Same for bassoons and trombone. And the Lahti hall is so clear. You can hear everything. And they can play pianissimo here. Of course, sometimes a piece that sounds good here doesn't sound so good in another hall."

Some have said that in Finland, because it had no court tradition and therefore no history of art sponsored by an elite aristocracy, its concert music has never strayed far from the taste of its public. Modernism, in other words, has never been especially rigorous in Finland. "That is true. As a result," Aho said, "when I started, it was easier because we didn't have so much of a tradition of modern music. I could create that tradition, as could other composers here at that time. We could do something that was never before done in Finland. That was good for us and gave us the feeling that what we were doing was important. It's much harder now for a young composer, because now modern music is quite strong. There are many very good composers here. So it's more difficult for young composers to find their own way, much more difficult than it was for me. And also because we don't have special audiences for modern music, you have to be able to write music that's not too complicated for the people."

To say, however, that Aho's music communicates doesn't mean that it's easy to play. R. Douglas Wright, principal trombone of the Minnesota Orchestra, first played the solo part in Aho's Symphony No. 9, subtitled Sinfonia Concertante No. 2, a work for trombone and orchestra, in several performances in Minnesota. An exuberantly imaginative work that alternates passages in a kind of stylized baroque with that of an expressionist idiom of the late twentieth century, the symphony makes great demands on the orchestra but especially on the soloist, who is asked to play a sackbut, an early version of the trombone, as well as his own modern instrument. Wright said he spent several months learning the solo part, which covers about five octaves. He described the big third-movement cadenza as "from another universe. Every piece of Aho's we've played is phenomenally difficult," Wright said. "Despite that, his music really does come from the heart. The difficulty is a means to an end rather than the end itself, and that makes the struggles in it worthwhile."

Vänskä, who has championed Aho's music for two decades, said, "Aho really goes to the edge. If someone says that this is the highest note for this instrument that you can write, he will take it even higher. His way of writing makes conductors crazy. Some orchestras have refused to play some of his music. They cancelled them and played something else. But when we started playing his music in Lahti, we found that if we do what he has written, the music will sound good. But it means work. Also, I always felt that his music was communicating something. It's not gray. He's not just writing for his colleagues. Some say it sounds like Shostakovich. I say, maybe, the early works. But why is that a negative? Gradually Aho found his own way. So often you have this big break or crash in his music, and then a softer section. The Violin Concerto is a good example. The ending gets so wild and violent, and when it finally crashes, you have this kind of angels' song. This is characteristic of his music, and I have liked it since the beginning. He is someone who is brave enough to write his own emotional ideas and open enough to tell the audience what he is feeling. Whereas what I call these gray composers are telling nothing about what happens in the heart. That's why I have always appreciated Kalevi. He isn't planning to do any kind of a show with spotlights. Instead, his music comes from inside."

What about Aho's reach as a composer? For whom does he write? Sibelius, who became a cultural hero in Finland, addressed the nation. Can any composer today make that claim? "Shostakovich was the last, I think, to do that," Aho said. "Maybe you need a big crisis in a society, as happened with Sibelius in the years leading to Finnish independence and in the two wars. Today that is difficult. Music today, at least classical music, doesn't have the

Kalevi Aho

function it had in Sibelius's time. Pop music has taken the role once fulfilled by classical music. Also, if you think about the problems in society, pop music can address them more directly and sooner, whereas, if I write a symphony that tells some of the problems in the world, it takes a year to compose and a year for the premiere, and so it's late. I have written operas, and they deal with the problems of the world."

Einojuhani Rautavaara

Einojuhani Rautavaara is the elder statesman of Finnish music. With his sharp wit, he says, "I was always slow. Everything I do is slow. I have a very large output, so many compositions. But to do that, I have to work every hour of the day. Nowadays I work an hour, then I rest." At this moment, he had six compositions in various stages of production, among them concertos for cello and percussion, a Catholic mass, and an opera on the life of the poet Federico Garcia Lorca. Asked if there is any thread linking Finnish music, Rautavaara mentioned an identification with nature and a predilection for meditative states. "I tell my colleagues," he said, "speaking about the slow movements of their works, that I always see before my eyes a typical Finnish farmer sitting outside after taking a sauna, looking at the lake and meditating about the deep things of life."

Einojuhani Rautavaara

In 2000, Osmo Vänskä conducted the Minnesota Orchestra in the premiere of Rautavaara's Harp Concerto with Kathy Kienzle as soloist. Rautavaara visited the Twin Cities for the occasion. He had come to the United States many years earlier to study composition at the Juilliard School and at Tanglewood, having received a scholarship through the recommendation of Jean Sibelius, then ninety years old. Sibelius had heard some of the young composer's work—Rautavaara

still isn't sure which pieces—and was impressed. It was while he was living in New York City that he learned to speak fluent English. He had with him the Finnish recording of his "Requiem," but failed to show it to the relevant people. "I've never been good at exploiting connections," he said. "I'm a lone wolf trotting through the forest."

Rautavaara's output of symphonies, operas, choral, piano, and solo vocal works span a wide stylistic spectrum, from serialism early in his career to a rich and highly individual postmodernism that combines elements of Mahler-like lushness with avant-garde and even ancient and folk elements. It is a diversity that Rautavaara defends: "If a composer writes in the same style at seventy as at twenty-five, he must be infantile," he said. "I started with music rather late, so I had a hard time learning all the techniques. The only way was to compose myself into those styles. What looked like experimenting was actually studying."

Though his career is now in its seventh decade, Rautavaara didn't begin to achieve international renown until the 1990s. The initial recognition, as happened with Vänskä, came through recordings. The Finnish label Ondine began to record nearly all of the composer's work, and he enjoyed a real hit with his Symphony No. 7, subtitled "Angels of Light." His most popular work remains his "Cantus Arcticus" (1972), a piece scored for the unusual combination of orchestra and birds—the bird sounds emanating from tape recordings. His Symphony No. 8, premiered by the Philadelphia Orchestra in 2000, enjoys a distinction rare among contemporary works, having already been recorded four times. Through all his changes in style, Rautavaara remains a mystic who thinks that his compositions already exist in "another reality," and that it is his function to bring them into the world in one piece. "It is my belief," he once said, "that music is great if, at some moment, the listener catches a glimpse of eternity through the window of time. This, to my mind, is the only true justification for all art. All else is of secondary importance."

Vänskä, who has recorded several of Rautavaara's works, including "Cantus Arcticus," said that Rautavaara's music is more lyrical than that of his countryman, Kalevi Aho. "This becomes more apparent in his later works, like the Seventh and Eighth Symphonies," Osmo said. "He was more this kind of, not angry, but direct composer earlier. But he found his style. 'Cantus Arcticus' is a good example, where the same theme is repeated with different colors. This later meditative style looks back but with modern harmonies. He's not doing nostalgia, in other words. And he's not a Shostakovich- or Prokofiev-style composer. I think this change also comes from a very happy time with his second wife, Sini. I know Sini, and he has been so happy with her. I think that comes out in his music. He didn't have any aggression anymore. He is a happy man."

And he has been happy with Vänskä. "Osmo is the one who always does exactly what the composer wants," said Rautavaara. "He does only what's in the score."

"The Sibelius was revelatory.
Vänskä restored the authentic Sibelian element of wildness,
the beauty and terror of nature,
and the awe that nature inspires in humankind.
Vänskä has real imagination, real understanding."
Richard Dyer, *Boston Globe*

Farewell to Lahti

From a distance at night, the splendid Sibelius Hall in Lahti shines like a glass lantern, an intricate mosaic of glass and wood illuminating the old harbor of Vesijärvi, at one time a flourishing inland port from which timber and other goods were shipped to St. Petersburg. Completed in 2000, the hall was quickly judged to be Finland's finest and perhaps the best concert hall in northern Europe. Both for the beauty of its design and the clarity of its acoustics, it is a fitting home for the Lahti Symphony Orchestra, which through its recordings and tours has put this modest-sized city of 100,000 on the cultural map, not just in Finland but throughout the world.

Whereas most concert halls stand firmly apart from nature, Lahti's Sibelius Hall seems like an extension of the natural world around it. It is the first modern concert hall to be built entirely of wood. Its central foyer, the Forest Hall, with its wood pylons and trusses that reach toward the heavens like the branches of a tree, aims to recall the atmosphere of a starlit pine forest, though the building's most magical touch can be observed in the ceiling. In a gesture toward Finland's central cultural figure, the alignment of the stars, realized with fiber optic cables, marks a special moment in time—the date of Sibelius's birth, December 8, 1865.

Most nights the hall is a hub of activity. And it is busy during the day, too. The hall is attached to what was once a furniture factory, a red brick structure put up in 1908 that is now used as a convention and conference center. The building also houses the orchestra's dressing and rehearsal rooms, technical facilities and staff offices, along with that indispensable Finnish institution: a large sauna allowing staff and musicians to sweat away their tensions and worries.

On this particular week in early May 2008, the activity was especially intense. In two concerts and a flurry of related events, Osmo Vänskä was saying goodbye to the Lahti Symphony Orchestra, stepping down as chief conductor after a twenty-three year association that began in 1985 when he was named principal guest conductor and then, three years later, chief conductor, the title he held for the ensuing two decades. By all accounts he was the right man at the right time. Under Vänskä's patient but determined guidance, the orchestra realized its dream, becoming an integral part of the community while rising from the status of provincial ensemble to that of a virtuosic orchestra with an international reputation. During that time Vänskä himself slowly but steadily emerged as one of the world's most admired conductors. Following these concerts Vänskä would devote himself to his full-time position as music director of the Minnesota Orchestra and to guest conducting.

Musicians whistled as they hurried from practice rooms to rehearsal. "This is a moment to celebrate what we've done," said Jaakko Kuusisto, the thirty-four-year-old concertmaster who joined the orchestra in 1999 and in recent years

Following these concerts Vänskä would devote himself to his full-time position as music director of the Minnesota Orchestra and to guest conducting.

has taken up conducting and composition. "Osmo is going on to very good things, and I'm confident the orchestra is going on to good things, too," he said.

Sibelius Hall was crowded for Osmo's last concert as principal conductor of the Lahti Symphony Orchestra.

Vänskä leaves the orchestra in good financial shape. "The Lahti Symphony has more sponsor money than any other Finnish orchestra, about fifteen percent of the budget," said Heikki Hakala, editor-in-chief of the city's daily newspaper, the *Etelä-Suomen Sanomat*. He has known Vänskä since they were children. "The rest comes from the city, the government, and box office."

Despite the party atmosphere, there is a sadness in the air of Sibelius Hall. Kuusisto said the whole idea of leave-taking hit him hardest just a few weeks earlier during the orchestra's brief tour to Poland, especially when Vänskä conducted a work so strongly identified with this orchestra and its conductor, Sibelius's Symphony No. 5. "That was a difficult performance for me," he said. "That's when I realized it's basically over."

All of Finland seemed to take notice. Vesa Sirén, the music critic of the *Helsinki Sanomat* and a veteran Vänskä observer wrote, "Someone may find his or her eyes watering today. Osmo Vänskä is conducting the Lahti Symphony for the last time."

Cellist Ilkka Uurtimo joined the orchestra in 1985, the same year that the management secured the services of a thirty-two-year-old, largely unknown but promising conductor, Osmo Vänskä, for the position of principal guest conductor. With two new people at the helm—Ulf Soderblom, chief conductor of the Finnish National Opera, had come aboard that same year as chief conductor—the orchestra was clearly inaugurating a new era, and the city approved. A Lahti official had written at the time, "It costs just as much to have a bad orchestra as a good one, so why don't we push for a good one?"

The Lahti Symphony Orchestra of today is a different orchestra than it was back then, Uurtimo said. "The sound is better. We read music better. We take responsibility better for our own parts. When I started here, we came in on Monday mornings and opened the music for the first time. That was the old system in Finland. We had a concert every two weeks. So there was plenty of time to learn the parts. Then when Osmo and Soderblom came, we started having two concerts a week. It became a different profession.

"Osmo has always had a vision of what he wants, a sound vision and a rhythmic vision," he said. "Those are the main themes of his conducting today, too. I have always liked Osmo. I like the way he works. He doesn't waste time. I think the way Osmo has fixed this engine is that it's very exact. I like Osmo's style of conducting. I wouldn't want to change Osmo."

He recalled the Garage Meetings that were initiated in the late 1980s as a way of encouraging a team spirit within the organization. Involving the musicians in the decision-making process was a bold idea back then. It became a point of discussion, if not an exact model, for American orchestras some years later. The Lahti meetings, which were actually held in a garage, were "a big success," Uutimo said. Kinberg remembers, however, that initially it wasn't easy to get musicians to open up about their feelings toward their work. "The old tradition was that musicians weren't supposed to have meetings and discussions," Kinberg said. "The idea was, 'We come, we play, and we go.' There's been a radical change here in the way people think about how they should be involved in the development of the orchestra."

At one point Kinberg asked the musicians to name their dreams for the orchestra. He wrote the ideas on a blackboard. One musician spoke up, saying that he wanted the orchestra, which had never made a commercial record, to make a CD that would be internationally recognized. Another wished for a good hall on a lakeside. (The orchestra's home at that time was a small hall in downtown Lahti with acoustics one musician described as "noisy.") A third hoped that some day people would fight for tickets when the orchestra played a concert in Helsinki. All of these utopias were realized.

Talk of a new hall for the orchestra had gone on for decades, but the talk stopped in the early 1990s when Lahti suffered a severe recession involving some thirty percent unemployment, due to the collapse of the Soviet Union which largely killed off exports to St. Petersburg from Lahti, especially the city's wood-working business. It was just a few years

later, however, that the concept of wood arose as the spark plug for what would become Sibelius Hall. The Finnish wood-processing giant Metsäliitto, hearing of the acclaim for the Lahti orchestra's landmark recording of Sibelius's tone poem "The Wood Nymph," expressed an interest in becoming one of the orchestra's sponsors. Moreover, because that very year, 1996, had been designated by Finland's prime minister the Year of Wood, it seemed to Kinberg and his team a bold but sensible plan to pitch the idea of a wooden concert hall in Lahti and for Metsäliitto to be the "guardian" of the venture.

The Ministry of Education joined in. The go-ahead finally came in May 1998, when the Lahti city council voted (30 to 29) to build the hall. The architects, winners of a year-long competition, were to be Kimmo Lintula and Hannu Tikka, and the acoustician for the project was Russell Johnson of Artec, an American firm. Vänskä led the orchestra on the hall's official opening night, March 10, 2000. It was an all-

Finnish program with works by Klami, Sibelius, Kokkonen and Aho—in fact, the premiere of Aho's Symphony No. 11.

Sibelius Hall is a vast improvement over its predecessor. Even so, the musicians had trouble adjusting to their new acoustical environment. "The orchestra wasn't happy at all," said Kinberg. "Some even thought things were better in the old hall. It took a couple of years for them to get over this. And, of course, bigger audiences meant bigger pressure and more concerts. The publicity was huge, and there were international guest artists every week. But because of these Garage Meetings, we had the tools to deal with this. We didn't need to invite a psychologist from outside to tell us what to do."

It was time for Vänskä to say goodbye to Lahti, and from Minnesota to greet the rest of the world.

And now, nearly a decade later, there can be no doubt that Sibelius Hall and the Lahti orchestra have given this city, once known chiefly as a haven for sports fans, a substantial cultural identity. Hakala recalls sitting in a bar in Tokyo chatting with two Japanese businessmen. When he told them he was from Finland, one said, "Finland—I know the Lahti orchestra." Said Hakala, "It turned out he had been to Finland several times for the annual Sibelius Festival we have here. He's such a fan of Sibelius's music."

Another orchestra veteran, bassist Timo Ahtinen, reminisced about his favorite tour performances and spoke of what this moment signified for him. On one of those tours the orchestra gave an outdoor concert in Alhambra that start-ed at 10:00 p.m. "I'll never forget it. We played the Sibelius Fifth Symphony under a starry sky," he said. Vänskä, he said, hasn't changed much over the years. "As a young conductor, he wasn't so economical in his gestures, but his attitude toward making music was the same as it is today. Of course, I know he is a star, but we've known each other for such a long time. He's like a family member who became a star. I'm sure when he comes back, he'll still be wearing one of his cozy t-shirts. It happens very seldom anymore that a conductor and an orchestra spend twenty-three years together. So, in that sense, it's upsetting that he's leaving. We've had such great times with him, with touring, with recording, with playing in our own hall. But that's how life goes. So I understand that maybe it's good for the orchestra and good for Osmo that we get new challenges. We have been, you know, in a sort of safe situation quite a long time. We know what to expect. It goes like a train. But I like very much when there's a little bit of pressure on people when they are working with music. You have to try. You have to think. You have to find new challenges and new interesting things, new ways to do things, and work all the time. We have had such good times. I'm happy for these years. In that way, I'm not sad. There are good ways to see the future. Let's see what happens."

Though this was a week for shared memories, Vänskä's farewell program embodied the present rather than the past. The curtain-raiser was the premiere of a work for percussion ensemble and orchestra by the Icelandic composer Askell Masson. The second half was devoted to Bruckner's Symphony No. 9, which, although composed in the nineteenth century, is a very up-to-date item in Vänskä's repertory.

The crowd that filed into the lobby at intermission was casually dressed—a lot of denim and open collars. This could be Minneapolis on a Thursday night at Orchestra Hall. Clearly, this wasn't a crowd bent on showing off. The city's cultural elite, someone said, will show up the following night.

Ages ranged from teens to elderly, though middle-aged was most common.

And, as it happened, there were quite a few Vänskäs in the audience, among them Osmo's oldest brother, Raimo, and his wife Marjatta. Joining them were several of Osmo's nieces and nephews and their spouses. They are children of the middle brother, Seppo, a Lutheran missionary who lives in Japan.

The Lahti auditorium is a space large enough to accommodate 1,250 people with no loss of intimacy. The feeling is communal, an appropriate aura in a country with such a strong sense of community. The balconies curve sensuously, and the color scheme is warm and inviting: reds in various shades mixed with lightly-colored smoked birch parquet and, on the seats, dark grey fabric. The thirty-ton acoustical canopy over the stage can be raised or lowered to modify the hall's acoustics, a device seen in many new halls these days. A more novel touch comes with the acoustic doors—188 of them—at balcony level that can be opened to adjust the hall's volume and reverberation time. Wood is everywhere. If there's a theme in the design, it's the creative use of wood.

And if wood, as the theory has it, resonates like a stringed instrument, then the auditorium of Sibelius Hall is like a fine old Stradivarius—an apt environment for the rich, organ-like sonorities of Bruckner's Symphony No. 9, which sounded forth in all its grandeur and mystery during the second half of the concert. Beyond that, Vänskä's carefully sustained tempos gave the music a sense of inevitability.

For the Thursday night concert the movers and shakers of Lahti were on hand to see and be seen and to pay their respects to a favorite son, a conductor who was now an international star. Hidden away in a hallway, to be presented at a post-concert dinner, was a sculpture in wood, "Vänskä's Gate," the work of a local artist, Markku Kosenon, a gift from the musicians and staff of the orchestra. Five poles were arranged against a back-drop so as to resemble a musical stave. Each pole carried its own meaning, the first being a symbol of artistic expression, the last taking the shape of a hay-pole, a symbol of Finland's farming culture. One of the evening's guests was the composer Kalevi Aho, who has enjoyed a long and fruitful relationship with Vänskä and the Lahti Symphony.

The Thursday evening concert was sold out. The music flowed effortlessly, and for a while, as happens in most great performances, time seemed to stop. Past and future were erased. There was only the present. The tender final moments for tenor tubas, horns, and strings stretched out, as if the music were reaching toward some indefinable goal in the distance. The music stopped finally, and there was a long pause—not a sound in the hall. Vänskä slowly lowered his arms, and the audience exploded with applause. Turning to face the audience, he looked shaken and drained of energy. He returned to the stage, gestured for the brass players to stand, bowed again, then walked off. He returned twice more. By then the audience was standing and cheering and clapping in rhythm. It was over.

Backstage, Kuusisto, responding to a compliment from an audience member, said, "Everyone wanted to give their best tonight," then moved on. A crowd had already gathered in the hall's Green Room—friends, colleagues, admirers, his wife Pirkko and two of the Vänskä children, Tytti and Perttu—to offer greetings and congratulations. Vänskä, as if not quite ready to meet them yet, stood alone outside his dressing room door, lost in thought. "In the last two minutes of the Bruckner, I just started to cry," he said. "I was thinking of the many concerts the orchestra and I did together." He paused, then moved on to greet the crowd.

It had been a long, unpredictable ride so far, and now it was to continue. It was time for Vänskä to say goodbye to Lahti, and from Minnesota to greet the rest of the world.

"Lahti was an
important time in my life.
But it was also good that I
was able to leave when I did.
It was time to look to the future.
And I'm so happy that I have
the Minnesota Orchestra.
I have a lot of opportunities
with this great orchestra."

Osmo Vänskä

Acknowledgments

We acknowledge the assistance and sometimes extensive help of many people who made contributions to this book. At the head of the list is Michael Anthony, former music critic for the Minneapolis *Star Tribune*, whose vast knowledge of classical music, the Minnesota Orchestra, and the international culture of orchestral conductors provided a background from which to do the necessary research. His acceptance of the task of producing a text resource for this book provided Osmo Vänskä an assurance that the book would have a professional integrity. If a single photo is worth a thousand words, the work of photographers Greg Helgeson and Ann Marsden, among others, have greatly expanded the message of this book. See page 127 for the photo acknowledgments.

Gwen Pappas, director of public relations for the orchestra, adopted the publisher's vision for this book and served as liaison to Osmo Vänskä as decisions were made and contracts signed. Her previous working relationship with Michael Anthony enabled her to gently guide and encourage as the writing was underway. She and Sandi Brown, public relations coordinator, read drafts of the manuscript and proofs. Ms. Brown made extra copies of manuscript drafts and guided the publisher through the vast photo library of the orchestra. Michael Pelton, executive assistant to the music director, who is, among other things, the keeper of the music director's schedule, was most cooperative in arranging meetings and interviews, and in the transmission of materials to and from Vänskä. As the project neared completion, Nicky Carpenter read the draft manuscript and wrote the insightful foreword.

WRITER ACKNOWLEDGMENTS

Michael Anthony acknowledges the following people who provided information and assistance in his preparation of the text resource for this book:

The hard-working orchestra librarians, Paul Gunther and Eric Sjostrom, who filled me in on their exacting work; stage manager Tim Eickholt, who pushed the right buttons, allowing me to record Osmo's voice during a week of rehearsals; marketing director Cindy Grzanowski, who shed so much light on the relevant numbers and stats; and personnel manager Julie Haight-Curran, the musicians' den mother, who shared tales of the orchestra. Among the many orchestra musicians who offered valuable thoughts and recollections were: Mischa Santora, Michael Sutton, Thomas Turner, Eiji Ikeda, Ben Ullery, David Wright, Janet Horvath, William Schrickel, Jonathan Magness, Wendy Williams, John Miller Jr., Manny Laureano, Charles Lazarus, R. Douglas Wright, Kari Sundström, Kathy Kienzle. And finally, deep appreciation to Jorja Fleezanis, concertmaster, who gave me an insightful, no-holds-barred interview. A special thank you to Sam Bergman, for the valuable blog he wrote during the 2004 tour of Europe, on which I drew heavily.

The hard-working co-directors of the orchestra's annual Composer Institute, Aaron Jay Kernis and Beth Cowart, explained this innovative program and their devotion to it. Many from the board shared their thoughts, notably the astute Luella Goldberg, while on the management side Robert R. Neu patiently answered every question I asked. And not least was former orchestra president David Hyslop, who kindly dug into his collection of dusty old calendars to set me straight on the chronology of Osmo's appointment.

Across the ocean, the Finns were no less helpful, and that includes the Vänskä nephews, nieces, and children (Tytti and Perttu). A special thank you to Osmo's brother Raimo, who graciously drove me to all the relevant places in Kotka, took me to see Osmo's mother, Maire, and, finally, joined by his wife, Marjatta, served at his home the best Finnish meal I had during ten days in that orderly country.

And no one knows more about the Finnish musical scene than Kai Amberla and the critic Vesa Sirén, both of whom gave generously of their time and their observations, as did Marjo Heiskanen of the Finnish Music Information Center. Two giants of Finnish music, Kalevi Aho and Einojuhani Rautavaara, offered wise and witty reflections on their music and on the musical world in general. In Lahti, there was a lively interview with Heikki Hakala, editor of the city's daily newspaper, followed by patient guidance and help from the busy staff of the Lahti Symphony, starting with general manager Tuomas Kinberg, his deputy, Teemu Kirjonaa, and the marketing director, Taina Räty, along with cellist Ilkka Uutimo, bassist Timo Ahtinen, and concertmaster Jaakko Kuusisto.

Osmo's manager, Lydia Connolly, gave me shrewd insight into the building of an international career, while the two members of the BIS recording team, producer Rob Suff and engineer Ingo Petry, gave me easy entry into the mysteries of the recording science—and art.

The one constant presence during the eighteen months of writing the text for this book was the indefatigable Mary Ann Feldman, friend, confidant, proofreader, scholar, and fellow-traveler, without whom the trip to Finland in May 2008 would have been considerably less productive. The bilingual Eeva Savolainen helped with translating Finnish. My neighbor and "tech guy," Jason Lake, not only kept my computer files in order but quickly responded to an emergency call one night when everything within reach crashed—including my hopes.

Finally, there was our star, our focus, our subject, our cynosure, Osmo Vänskä. Cajoled into this project by the intrepid publisher, Leonard Flachman, Osmo turned out to be an ideal subject: attentive, informed and with a good sense of humor. Talking about oneself for eleven hours—eleven one-hour interviews stretching over the course of eight months—isn't one's idea of a good time. But, Osmo, the gentleman, responded beautifully.

PHOTOGRAPHY ACKNOWLEDGMENTS

Greg Helgeson: pages 6, 10, 11, 13, 18, 19, 24, 25, 27, 55, 58, 59, 61, 62, 63, 65, 67, 68, 69, 70, 71, 80, 85, 86, 87, 89, 90, 91, 92, 93, 94, 95, 96, 97, 98, 99, 100, 103, 108, 121, 122.

Ann Marsden: cover, pages 8, 12, 21, 26, 54, 83, 104, 107, 111, 124.

Travis Anderson: page 79, 82.

Eric Moore: page 53.

Tim Rummelhoff, page 125.

Osmo Vänskä: pages 30, 32, 33, 34, 35, 36, 44, 49, 50, 51, 52.

Lahti Symphony Orchestra: pages 40, 41, 42, 47, 105, 118, 120.

Helsinki Philharmonic Orchestra: pages 37, 39.

BBC Scottish Symphony Orchestra
    Drew Farrell: page 45.
    Eric Thorburn: page 46.

Discography

AHO, Kalevi

Symphony No. 1
Silence
Violin Concerto
BIS CD 396
Lahti Symphony Orchestra/Manfred Gräsbeck

Symphonies No.. 2 & 7
BIS CD 936
Lahti Symphony Orchestra

Symphony No. 3
BIS CD 1186
Lahti Symphony Orchestra/Matti Salminen

Symphony No. 4
Chinese Songs
BIS CD 1066
Lahti Symphony Orchestra/Tiina Vahevaara

Symphony No. 8 for organ and orchestra
Pergamon
BIS CD 646
Lahti Symphony Orchestra/Hans-Ola Ericsson/
    Lilli Paasikivi/Eeva-Liisa Saarinen/Ton
    Nyman/Matti Lehtinen/Pauli Pietiläinen

Symphony No. 9 for trombone and orchestra
Concerto for cello and orchestra
BIS CD 706
Lahti Symphony Orchestra/Christian Lindberg/
    Gary Hoffman

Symphony No. 10
Rejoicing of the Deep Waters
BIS CD 856
Lahti Symphony Orchestra

Symphony No.11
Symphonic Dances
BIS CD-1336
Lahti Symphony Orchestra/Kroumata Percussion
    Ensemble

BEETHOVEN, Ludwig van

Symphony No. 7
BBCP1005-2
BBC Scottish Symphony

Symphonies Nos. 2 and 7
SACD-1816
Minnesota Orchestra

Symphonies Nos. 1 and 6
SACD-1716
Minnesota Orchestra

Symphony No. 9 "Choral"
SACD-1616
Minnesota Orchestra

Symphonies Nos. 3 and 8
SACD-1516
Minnesota Orchestra

Symphonies Nos. 4 and 5
SACD-1416
Minnesota Orchestra

Sinfonietta
Serenade for tenor, horn & strings
Now Sleeps the Crimson Petal
BIS CD 540
Tapiola Sinfonietta/Christoph Prégardien/
    Lanzky-Otto

BRUCKNER, Anton
Symphony No. 3 (1876 version)
CDA67200
BBC Scottish Symphony

CRUSELL, Bernard Henrik
Three Clarinet Concertos
BIS CD 345
Lahti Symphony Orchestra/Karl Leister

Introduction and Swedish Air for clarinet and
    orchestra
Sinfonia Concertante
BIS CD 495
Tapiola Sinfonietta/Anna-Maija Korsima-Hursti,
    László Hara, Ib Lanzky-Otto

Three Clarinet Quartets
BIS CD 741
Osmo Vänskä, Pekka Kauppinen, Anu Airas, and
    Ilkka Pälli

GUBAIDULINA, Sofia
Concerto for bassoon and low strings
Concordanza for instrumental ensemble
Detto II for cello and chamber ensemble
BIS CD 636
Lahti Chamber Ensemble/Harri Ahmas/Ilkka
     Pälli

KANAJUS, Robert
Finnish Rhapsody No. 1
Kullervo's Funeral March
Sinfonietta
BIS CD 1223
Lahti Symphony Orchestra

KOKKONEN, Jonas
Volume I (Symphonic Sketches, Concerto for
     cello and piano, Symphony No. 4)
BIS CD 468
Lahti Symphony Orchestra/Torleif Thedéen

Volume III (Inauguratio Interludes from the Last
     Temptations, Erekhtheion, Symphony No. 2)
BIS CD 498
Lahti Symphony Orchestra/Satu Vihavainen/
     Walton Grönroos/Akateeminen Laulu Choir

Volume V (Sinfonia da camera, Il paesaggio,
     Wind Quintet)
BIS CD 528
Lahti Symphony Orchestra/Ulf Söderblom/
     Sinfonia Lahti Wind Quintet

The Four Symphonies
Opus Sonorum
Sinfonia da camera
Requiem
BIS CD 849.5
Lahti Symphony Orchestra/Ilkka Sivonen/Soile
     Isokoski/Walton Grönroos/Savonlinna Opera
     Festival Choir/Ulf Söderblom

KLAMI, Uuno
Pyörteitä ballet, suites 1 & 2
Lemminkäinen's Island Adventures
Song of Lake Kuujärvi
BIS CD 656
Lahti Symphony Orchestra/Esa Ruuttunen

The Cobblers on the Heath
Theme with seven variations and coda for cello
     and orchestra
Kalavala Suite
BIS CD 676
Lahti Symphony Orchestra/Jan-Erik Gustafsson

Pyörteitä Ballet, Act I
Violin Concerto
Suomenlinna
BIS CD 696
Lahti Symphony Orchestra/Jennifer Koh

LEIFS, Jon
Saga Symphony
BIS CD 730
Iceland Symphony Orchestra

Geysir
Trilogia Piccola
Overture to "Loftr"
Trois peintures abstraites
Consolation-Intermezzo for strings
BIS CD 830
Iceland Symphony Orchestra

MAHLER, Gustav
Das Lied von der Erde (chamber orchestra version)
BIS CD 681
Sinfonia Lahti Chamber Ensemble/Monica
     Groop/Jorma Silvasti

MacMILLAN, James
The World's Ransoming
Cello Concerto
BIS CD 989
BBC Scottish Symphony/Raphael Wallfisch/
     Christine Pendrill

Symphony "Vigil"
BIS CD 990
BBC Scottish Symphony/Fine Arts Brass
     Ensemble

The Confession of Isobel Gowdie
Tuireadh (for clarinet and string orchestra)
The Exorcism of Rio Sumpúl
BIS CD 1169
BBC Scottish Symphony/Martin Fröst

MARTTINEN, Tuano
Symphonies Nos. 1 & 8
Concerto for violin and orchestra
BIS CD 701
Lahti Symphony Orchestra/Pekka Kauppinen

MUSSORGSKY, Modest
Songs of Death (arranged by Kalevi Aho)
BIS CD 1186
Lahti Symphony Orchestra/Matti Salminen

NIELSEN, Carl
Symphonies Nos. 1 & 6
BIS CD 1079
BBC Scottish Symphony

Symphonies Nos. 3 & 4
BIS CD 1209
BBC Scottish Symphony/Anu Komsi/Christian
     Immler

Symphonies Nos. 2 & 5
BIS CD 1289
Lahti Symphony Orchestra

PACIUS, Fredrik
Die Loreley: Opera in Two Acts
BIS CD 1393/94
Lahti Symphony Orchestra

PAGANINI, Niccolo
Violin Concerto No. 1
La Campanella for violin and piano
Cantabile for violin and piano
Moses Fantaszy for violin and piano
BIS CD 999
Iceland Symphony Orchestra/Ilya Gringolts

PAULUS, Stephen
To Be Certain of the Dawn
BIS SACD 1726
Minnesota Orchestra

PIZZETTI, Ildebrando
Rondo Veneziano
Preludio a un altro giorno
Tre Preludii Sinfonici
La Pisanella
CDA67084
BBC Scottish Symphony

POULENC, Francis
Complete Works for Two Pianos
Concerto for Two Pianos
Sonata for Two Pianos
Sonata for Piano four hands
BIS CD 593
Malmö Symphony Orchestra/Roland Pöntinen/
    Love Derwinger

RAUTAVAARA, Einojuhani
Symphony No. 7 "Angel of Light"
Dances with the Winds (concerto for flutes and
    orchestra)
Cantus arcticus (concerto for birds and orchestra)
BIS CD 1038
Lahti Symphony Orchestra/Petri Alanko

Violin Concerto
Symphony No. 8
BIS CD 1315
Lahti Symphony Orchestra/Petri Alanko

SALLINEN, Aulis
Variations for Orchestra
Violin Concerto
The Nocturnal Dances of Don Juan Quixote
BIS CD 560
Tapiola Sinfonietta/Eeva Koskinen/Torleif
    Thedéen

SANDSTRÖM, Jan
Emperor's Chant for trombone and orchestra
Trombone Concerto No. 2 "Don Quixote"
A Short Ride on a Motorbike for trombone and
    orchestra
BIS CD 828
Lahti Symphony Orchestra/Christian Lindberg

SIBELIUS, Jean
Rondo of Waves – Oceanides and more pieces
BIS CD 1445
Lahti Symphony Orchestra

Kullervo
BIS CD 1215
Lahti Symphony Orchestra/Lilli Paasikivi/Raimo
    Laukka/Helsinki University Chorus

Violin Concerto (original 1903-04 version)
Violin Concerto (final 1905 version)
BIS CD 500
Lahti Symphony Orchestra/Leonidas Kavakos

The Wood Nymph
A Lonely Ski-Trail
Swanwhite, incidental music (complete original
    score)
BIS CD 815
Lahti Symphony Orchestra/Lasse Pöysti

Symphonies Nos. 1 & 4
BIS CD 861
Lahti Symphony Orchestra

Symphonies Nos. 2 & 3
BIS CD 862
Lahti Symphony Orchestra

Symphony No. 5 (original 1915 version)
En Saga (original 1892 version)
BIS CD 800
Lahti Symphony Orchestra

Symphony No. 5 (original & final versions)
BIS CD 863
Lahti Symphony Orchestra

Symphonies No. 6 & 7
Tapiola
BIS CD 864
Lahti Symphony Orchestra

Karelia (world premiere recording)
Kuolema (world premiere recording)
Valse triste (final version)
BIS CD 915
Lahti Symphony Orchestra/Kirsi Tiihonen/
    Raimo Laukka/Heikki Lattinen/Taito Hoffren

Karelia Suite (original score)
King Christian II, incidental music
Pelléas et Mélisande (complete theatre version)
BIS CD 918
Lahti Symphony Orchestra/Raimo Laukka/Anna-
    Lisa Jakobsson

The Tempest
BIS CD 581
Lahti Symphony Orchestra

Jedermann/Everyman
Belshazzar's Feast
Incidental music (complete original version)
The Countess's Portrait
BIS CD 735
Lahti Symphony Orchestra/Lilli Paasikivi/Petri
    Lehto/Sauli Tiilikainen/Lahti Chamber
    Choir/Pauli Pietiläinen/Leena Saarenpää

Lemminkäinen Suite
BIS CD 1015
Lahti Symphony Orchestra

Patriotic Music: Press Celebrations Music
The Melting of the Ice on the Uleå River
A Song for Lemminkäinen
Have You Courage?
Song of the Athenians
BIS CD 1115
Lahti Symphony Orchestra/Helsinki University
    Chorus/Lasse Pöysti/Lahti Boys Choir

Finlandia
The Swan of Tuonela
Tapiola
Suite for Violin and String Orchestra
Valse triste
Spring Song
Alla Marcia from "Karelia Suite"
BIS CD 1125
Lahti Symphony Orchestra/Dong-Suk Kang

En Saga
The Dryad
Dance-Intermezzo
Pohjola's Daughter
Night Ride and Sunrise
The Bard
The Oceanides
BIS CD 1225
Lahti Symphony Orchestra

Complete Seven Symphonies
BIS CD 1286.88
Lahti Symphony Orchestra

The Voice of Sibelius
BIS CD 1433
Lahti Symphony Orchestra

The Sibelius Edition Vol. 1
Tone Poems
BIS CD 1900/02
Lahti Symphony Orchestra

The Sibelius Edition Vol. 3
Voice & Orchestra
BIS CD 1906/08
Lahti Symphony Orchestra

The Sibelius Edition Vol. 5
Orchestral Music for the Theatre
BIS CD 1912/14
Lahti Symphony Orchestra

The Origin of Fire
BIS CD 1525
Lahti Symphony Orchestra/YL Male Voice
    Choir/Tom Nyman/Tommi Hakala

In memoriam (first version)
Two Serious Melodies
Presto for strings
Lemminkäinen in Tuonela
Humoresque No.1
Three Pieces for Orchestra, Op.96
In memoriam (revised version)
BIS CD 1485
Lahti Symphony Orchestra

Spirit of Nature
Songs, Cantatas and Orchestral Works
BIS CD 1565
Lahti Symphony Orchestra

Finlandia
Karelia Suite
Violin Concerto in D minor
The Oceanides
Valse Triste
Andante festivo
En saga
Pohjolas´s Daughter
The Wood-Nymph
Tapiola
Porilaisten Marssi
BIS CD 1557/5
Lahti Symphony Orchestra/Leonidos Kavakos

Song of the Earth
The Captive Queen
Two Chorales
Promotional Cantata
Scout March
Hymn of the Earth
Processional
BIS CD 1365
Lahiti Symphony Orchestra/Juntunen/Hostikka

Snöfrid
Overture in A minor
Cantata for the Coronation of Nicholas II
Rakastava
Oma maa
Andante Festivo
BIS CD 1265
Lahti Symphony Orchestra

Finlandia
Excerpt from Symphony No.1
Excerpt from Suite in E major
Excerpt from Sonata in F from Symphony No.1
Excerpts from Karelia
The Swan of Tuonela
Valse triste from Symphony No.2
BIS CD 1295
Lahti Symphony Orchestra

SHOSTAKOVICH, Dmitri
Symphony No. 3
BBCP1005-2
BBC Scottish Symphony/London Symphony
    Chorus

VARIOUS
All the Lonely People (trombone concertos by
    Rimsky-Korsakov, Tomasi, Rota, Schnittke, and
    Rabe)
BIS CD 568
Tapiola Sinfonietta/Christian Lindberg

Finlandia — A Festival of Finnish Music (music of
    Sibelius, Raitie, Krohn, Rautavaara, etc.)
BIS CD 575
Lahti Symphony Orchestra/Dong-Suk Kang

Finnish Hymns I
BIS CD 1149
Lahti Symphony Orchestra

Finnish Hymns II
BIS CD 1349
Lahti Symphony Orchestra

Finnish Hymns III
BIS CD 1369
Lahti Symphony Orchestra

Finnish Folk Songs
BIS CD 1327
Lahti Symphony Orchestra

Finnish Flute Concertos (by Rautavaara,
    Bashmakov, Sallinen, and Marttinen)
BIS CD 687
Lahti Symphony Orchestra/Petri Alanko

Lahti Christmas
BIS CD 947
Lahti Symphony Orchestra/Laulupuu Choir of
    Lahti

Lahti Folk Songs
BIS CD 1327
Lahti Symphony Orchestra

Nordic Trombone Concertos (by Lindberg,
    Holmboe, Larsson, and Aho)
BIS CD 888
Lahti Symphony Orchestra/Christian Lindberg

"The Romantic Piano Concerto"
Romantisches Klavierkonzert (Marx)
Piano Concerto for the left hand (Korngold)
CDA66990
BBC Scottish Symphony/Marc-André Hamelin

Nielsen & Aho Clarinet Concertos
BIS SACD 1463
Lahti Symphony Orchestra/Martin Fröst

Swedish Hymns
BIS CD 1409
Lahti Symphony Orchestra

"Fiery, elegant, bristling with character—this is impressive Beethoven. . . .
The Minnesota Orchestra are extraordinarily proficient:
fleet-footed and articulate."

Richard Osborne, *Gramophone Magazine*

Orchestra Roster 2008-2009

Osmo Vänskä, *Music Director*

Stanislaw Skrowaczewski, *Conductor Laureate*

Andrew Litton, *Artistic Director, Sommerfest*
　　Marilyn Nelson Chair

Doc Severinsen, *Pops Conductor Laureate*

Dominick Argento, *Composer Laureate*

Aaron Jay Kernis, *New Music Advisor*

Mischa Santora, *Associate Conductor*

Sarah Hicks, *Assistant Conductor*

Minnesota Chorale, *Principal Chorus*

Kathy Saltzman Romey, *Choral Advisor*

Irvin Mayfield, *Artistic Director, Jazz*

FIRST VIOLINS

Jorja Fleezanis, *Concertmaster*
　　Elbert L. Carpenter Chair

Sarah Kwak, *First Associate Concertmaster*
　　Lillian Nippert and Edgar F. Zelle Chair

Roger Frisch, *Associate Concertmaster*
　　Frederick B. Wells Chair

Stephanie Arado, *Assistant Concertmaster*
　　Loring M. Staples, Sr., Chair

Pamela Arnstein

David Brubaker

Helen Chang

Rebecca Corruccini

Céline Leathead

Rudolf Lekhter

Peter McGuire

Chouhei Min

Joanne Opgenorth

Vali Phillips

Milana Elise Reiche

Deborah Serafini

SECOND VIOLINS

Gina DiBello, *Principal*
　　Sumner T. McKnight Chair

Jonathan Magness, *Associate Principal*

Julie Ayer, *Assistant Principal*

Taichi Chen

Jean Marker De Vere

Laurel Green

Aaron Janse

Kristin Kemper

Arnold Krueger

Catherine Schaefer Schubilske

Edward Stack

Michael Sutton

David Wright

VIOLAS
Thomas Turner, *Principal*
 Reine H. Myers Chair
Richard Marshall, *Co-Principal*
 Douglas and Louise Leatherdale Chair
Matthew Young, *Acting Assistant Principal*
Michael Adams
Sam Bergman
Sifei Cheng
Kenneth Freed
Eiji Ikeda
Megan Tam
Ben Ullery
Jennifer Strom*

CELLOS
Anthony Ross, *Principal*
 John and Elizabeth Bates Cowles Chair
Janet Horvath, *Associate Principal*
 John and Barbara Sibley Boatwright Chair
Beth Rapier, *Assistant Principal*
 Marion E. Cross Chair
Eugena Chang
Mina Fisher
Sachiya Isomura
Katja Linfield
Marcia Peck
Open
 Roger and Cynthia Britt Chair
Arek Tesarczyk

BASSES
Open, *Principal*
 Jay Phillips Chair
Fora Baltacıgil, *Acting Principal*
William Schrickel, *Acting Associate Principal*
 Mr. and Mrs. Edward E. Stepanek Chair
David Williamson, *Acting Assistant Principal*
Robert Anderson

Matthew Frischman
Brian Liddle
Michael Fuller*

FLUTES
Adam Kuenzel, *Principal*
 Eileen Bigelow Chair
Open, *Associate Principal*
 Henrietta Rauenhorst Chair
Wendy Williams
Roma Duncan Kansara

PICCOLO
Roma Duncan Kansara
 Alene M. Grossman Chair

OBOES
Basil Reeve, *Principal*
 Grace B. Dayton Chair
John Snow, *Associate Principal*
Julie Gramolini
Marni J. Hougham

ENGLISH HORN
Marni J. Hougham
 John Gilman Ordway Chair

CLARINETS
Burt Hara, *Principal*
 I. A. O'Shaughnessy Chair
Gregory T. Williams, *Associate Principal*
 Ray and Doris Mithun Chair
David Pharris
Timothy Zavadil

E-FLAT CLARINET
Gregory T. Williams

BASS CLARINET
Timothy Zavadil

BASSOONS
John Miller, Jr., *Principal*
  Norman B. Mears Chair
Mark Kelley, *Co-Principal*
  Marjorie F. and George H. Dixon Chair
J. Christopher Marshall
Norbert Nielubowski

CONTRABASSOON
Norbert Nielubowski

HORNS
Michael Gast, *Principal*
  John Sargent Pillsbury Chair
Herbert Winslow, *Associate Principal*
  Gordon C. and Harriet D. Paske Chair
Brian Jensen
Ellen Dinwiddie Smith
David Kamminga

TRUMPETS
Manny Laureano, *Principal*
  Mr. and Mrs. Archibald G. Bush Chair
Douglas C. Carlsen, *Associate Principal*
  Rudolph W. and Gladys Davis Miller Chair
Robert Dorer
Charles Lazarus

TROMBONES
R. Douglas Wright, *Principal*
  Star Tribune Chair
Kari Sundström
  William C. and Corinne J. Dietrich Chair

BASS TROMBONE
David Herring

TUBA
Steven Campbell, *Principal*
  Robert Machray Ward Chair

TIMPANI
Peter Kogan, *Principal*
  Dimitri Mitropoulos Chair
Jason Arkis, *Associate Principal*

PERCUSSION
Brian Mount, *Principal*
  WAMSO Chair
Jason Arkis, *Associate Principal*
  Opus Chair
Kevin Watkins

HARP
Kathy Kienzle, *Principal*
  Bertha Boynton Bean Chair

PIANO, HARPSICHORD AND CELESTA
Open, *Principal*
  Markell C. Brooks Chair

LIBRARIANS
Paul Gunther, *Principal*
Eric Sjostrom, *Associate Principal*
Open, *Assistant Principal*

PERSONNEL MANAGER
Julie Haight-Curran

ASSOCIATE PERSONNEL MANAGER
Leah Mohling

STAGE MANAGER
Timothy Eickholt

ASSISTANT STAGE MANAGERS
Gail Reich
Dave McKoskey

AUDIO ENGINEER
Terry Tilley

* *Replacement*